Library of
Davidson College

Also by Adam Carlyle Breckenridge

The Right to Privacy

Congress Against the Court

Adam Carlyle Breckenridge

UNIVERSITY OF NEBRASKA PRESS · LINCOLN

Publishers on the Plains

UNP

Copyright © 1970 by the University of Nebraska Press
All Rights Reserved
International Standard Book Number 0–8032–0751–4
Library of Congress Catalog Card Number 79–113168

347.9
B829c

73-7632

Manufactured in the United States of America

Contents

Preface

In *The Federalist* No. 81, Alexander Hamilton wrote:

> That there ought to be one court of supreme and final jurisdiction, is a proposition which is not likely to be contested. . . . The only question that seems to have been raised concerning it, is, whether it ought to be a distinct body or a branch of the legislature. . . . A legislature, without exceeding its province, cannot reverse a determination once made in a particular case; though it may prescribe a new rule for future cases.

This volume is related to these expressions by Hamilton. Efforts were made in the Ninetieth Congress, 1967–68, to challenge the U.S. Supreme Court as one of independent and final jurisdiction, and also to extend the power of Congress to prescribe rules for judicial observance.

The issues between these two branches of government involved a relatively small number of decisions by the high court in the area of the administration of justice—all during the terms of the Court headed by Chief Justice Earl Warren. These decisions affected many long-standing practices and procedures in federal and state law enforcement and in judicial proceedings, especially in the admission of confessions or statements in evidence at a trial, the speed with which an accused would be arraigned, and the right to counsel. Along with some which were unrelated, these decisions produced more than a decade of rising opposition to the Warren Court.

Supporters of the Court and the Warren leadership applauded the controversial decisions, claiming great advances in strengthening the constitutional rights of the individual.

But racial issues, unrest in urban areas, large and small, reports of a substantial rise in crime, a growing concern about many social and economic conditions in the nation, all helped climax a near-constitutional crisis. Unlike the Roosevelt court-packing plan, the Congress sought to overrule the objectionable decisions through legislation. The extent to which these efforts succeeded is given in the following pages.

Since the enactment in 1968 of the Omnibus Crime Control and Safe Streets Act, a new chief justice has been appointed and a replacement of an associate justice has been made. Others will follow. These changes in court personnel may produce even more changes as the remade Court reassesses the controversial Warren Court decisions than came from the legislative product of 1968.

Congress Against the Court

I

Introduction

————◆————

When President Lyndon B. Johnson signed H.R. 5037 in June, 1968, and with announced reluctance over some of its provisions, he climaxed another chapter in a series of conflicts among the three branches of government. The measure, however, dramatized sharply defined issues between two of the branches, the Congress and the U.S. Supreme Court, over the question of how to deal effectively in crime control and the administration of justice. This legislation, known as the Omnibus Crime Control and Safe Streets Act of 1968,[1] is not an ordinary piece of legislation; it is far-reaching, and may result in a major extension of the national government into what has long been considered the province of the states and their local governments, i.e., the responsibility for the general enforcement of criminal laws. The statute is intended, as specifically announced by its supporters, to overrule some U.S. Supreme Court decisions, and for the first time authorizes law enforcement officers in all levels of government to engage in electronic surveillance—wire tapping and "bugging." Its long-range effects are still to be determined, as are tests of constitutionality, but among the possibilities are a greater degree of uniformity among the states in the detection and apprehension procedures affecting those who may be involved in criminal acts. It could provide the avenue for greater uniformity in criminal prosecutions, definitions of crimes, and sentences.

1. Public Law 90-351 of June 19, 1968.

The Omnibus Crime Act had its formal beginnings in the president's State of the Union message of January 10, 1967, and his special message of February 6, the same year.[2]

The substance of these messages as related to crime had roots in the report of the president's Commission on Law Enforcement and Administration of Justice, issued as of February 18, 1967, entitled "The Challenge of Crime in a Free Society." The president's special message was prefaced with this statement:

> In our democracy, the principal responsibility for dealing with crime does not lie with the National Government, but with the States and local communities. . . . Yet . . . the Federal Government has accepted a substantial responsibility . . . augmenting State and local efforts . . . to pay increased attention to its role in the control of crime.

He then proceeded to set the stage for his safe streets and crime control act emphasizing that

> the Federal Government must not and will not try to dominate the system. It could not if it tried. Our system of law enforcement is essentially local; based upon local initiative, generated by local energies, and controlled by local officials. But the Federal Government must help to strengthen the system, and to encourage the kind of innovations needed to respond to the problem of crime in America.

The essential features of the president's proposal were to (1) provide planning and program grants to the states and local governments; (2) establish, in the Department of Justice, a director of a new Office of Law Enforcement and Criminal Justice Assistance; (3) provide grants to states, cities, and regional and metropolitan bodies to assist them in developing plans to improve their police, courts, and correctional systems; (4) authorize the attorney general to make research grants or

2. See *House Document* No. 53, 90th Cong., 1st sess. It is included in *Hearings before Subcommittee No. 5 of the Committee on the Judiciary*, 90th Cong., 1st sess. (1967), pp. 1541–1549.

contracts with public agencies, institutions of higher education, or other organizations; and (5) authorize grants for the construction of significant new types of physical facilities, on a regional or metropolitan basis, such as crime laboratories, community correction centers, and police academy-type centers. The proposal had other features including firearms control, drug control, and the extension of immunity to witnesses.

Some of the local and regional programs suggested which might qualify for grants were those which would provide:

Better training for criminal justice personnel
Various innovative techniques, such as tactical squads, special
    street lighting, new public alarm systems
More effective alarm systems
Two-way radio and multiple-channel police networks
Coordinate information systems for all law and correction
    officials
New rehabilitation techniques and personnel to employ them
Salaries for criminal justice personnel where associated with
    special training or innovative programs

It was also proposed that plans to implement the above meet certain qualifying tests. These included a minimum population jurisdiction of not less than 50,000, deal with all law enforcement in the area (with some exceptions), establish priorities, incorporate innovations and advanced techniques, and indicate evidence that state and local governments would assume the costs after a reasonable period of federal assistance.

The bill which reached the president nearly a year and a half later was a much broader piece of legislation, retaining most of his proposals, which was a victory in principle, but control over the use of funds would go to the states by block grants. Additional features which the president opposed included wire-tapping authorizations, sections intended to alter rulings of the U.S. courts, especially the Supreme Court in certain criminal justice areas, and less stringent controls over guns than he had hoped to obtain.

In the interval of nearly eighteen months before passage of the crime bill there was open and spirited attack on the U.S. Supreme Court. The milder House version—essentially the president's proposals—was cast aside when the House accepted the Senate version on June 6, 1968, the day of the death of Senator Robert F. Kennedy.

The crime bill was denounced by its critics during debate in the Senate as starting the nation down the road toward a government by police state procedures and one making a court-packing scheme. But its supporters claimed it would put the nation "back to law and the Constitution as they were before the Court undertook to liberalize them to the point that today it is becoming almost a rule of the Court that it find some technicality to release back on society, habitual, confirmed, and confessed criminals." [3]

Senator John L. McClellan (Dem.) of Arkansas, as chairman of the subcommittee of the Senate Committee on the Judiciary, set the tone for his participation in getting favorable action with reference to decisions of the U.S. Supreme Court, saying

> there is no question that these decisions have resulted in the freeing of multitudes of criminals of undoubted guilt and have unduly hampered legitimate law enforcement activities. The situation must be rectified and the duty to do so devolves rightly upon the Congress. [4]

Three U.S. Supreme Court decisions were pinpointed as being especially objectionable. These were *Mallory* v. *U.S.*,[5] decided in 1957, holding that arraignment must be made without unnecessary delay; *Miranda* v. *Arizona*,[6] decided in 1966, holding that an accused had to be advised of his rights before interrogation; and *U.S.* v. *Wade*,[7] decided in 1967,

3. *Congressional Record*, 90th Cong., 2nd sess., May 2, 1968, 11600.
4. *Hearings before the Subcommittee on Criminal Laws and Procedures of the Committee on the Judiciary, U.S. Senate*, 90th Cong., 1st sess. (1967), p. 5.
5. 354 U.S. 449.
6. 384 U.S. 436.
7. 388 U.S. 218.

holding that an accused had to have the right to counsel in police line-ups. Senator McClellan and his chief supporter, Senator Sam J. Ervin, Jr. (Dem.) of North Carolina, did not have a complete victory, however, because they tried without success to prevent the federal courts including the U.S. Supreme Court from reviewing "or to reverse, vacate, modify, or disturb in any way, a ruling of any trial court of any State in any criminal prosecution admitting in evidence as voluntarily made an admission or confession of an accused if such ruling has been affirmed or otherwise upheld by the highest court of the State having appellate jurisdiction of the cause."[8] A similar provision would have affected eyewitness testimony. Finally, although not at issue in *Mallory*, *Miranda*, or *Wade*, but directly related, an effort was made to prevent the use of a federal writ of habeas corpus in appeals from state cases where postconviction relief was sought. But the Senate refused to accept these severe restrictions.

Title II of the crime bill (Senate version, S. 917) was the vehicle by which the efforts were directed to overrule the U.S. Supreme Court. The bill, as finally passed, concerned the admissibility of confessions, some aspects of the right to counsel, and the use of eyewitness testimony. In this legislation, the Congress attempted to alter judicial interpretations of the Fifth, Sixth, and Fourteenth Amendments. Hearings were held by subcommittees of both houses in 1967. The resulting testimony consumed 1551 pages in the House and 1205 pages in the Senate.

The debates took place during both sessions of the Congress in the House and the second session in the Senate. There was sharp discourse between proponents and opponents. Judges, especially state judges, were highly critical of several Supreme Court holdings as being liberal in behalf of the accused and contrary to the public interest. Law enforcement officials at state and local levels and district attorneys of the United States were forceful in their view that the high court was soft

8. Section 3502, Title II, Senate Committee on the Judiciary version of S. 917, 90th Cong., 2nd sess., April 29, 1968.

on criminals and had placed, by its decisions, unreasonable and unwarranted restraints and requirements upon them so as to render their work difficult to impossible.[9]

As the debate ended in the House on June 5, 1968, Judiciary Committee chairman Emanuel Celler (Dem.) of New York called the legislation "a cruel hoax on citizens for whom crime and the fear of crime are the facts of life . . . . It is built on false premises. Its promises are illusory. It is destructive of the tenets of our liberty."[10] Minority Leader Gerald R. Ford (Rep.) of Michigan, however, echoed the majority view of the House, saying, "I refuse, Mr. Speaker, to concede that the elected representatives of the American people cannot be the winner in a confrontation with the Supreme Court."[11]

This was the atmosphere which prevailed during the hearings and the debate, and which has existed since on the Omnibus Crime Act of 1968. It was generated mostly by a

9. J. Edgar Hoover, director of the Federal Bureau of Investigation, was restrained in his comments in 1966 and 1967. See his statement in the FBI *Law Enforcement Bulletin* for September, 1966, and March, 1967. But the March, 1969, issue contained these words in his column: "A newspaper columnist noted that today's law enforcement officer has to 'speak softly and carry a big law library.'"

10. *Congressional Record*, 90th Cong., 2nd sess., June 5, 1968, 16066.

11. Critics of the Warren Court seldom recognize a number of recent decisions which greatly aided the work of law enforcement officers. Some involved reversals of earlier decisions. Examples are: *Warden* v. *Hayden*, 387 U.S. 294 (1967), which eliminated the distinction between seizure of items of evidential value only and seizure of instrumentalities, fruits, or contraband; *Hoffa* v. *U.S.* 387 U.S. 231 (1967), which rejected the argument that police could not use paid informers; *McCray* v. *Illinois*, 386 U.S. 300 (1967), holding that the name of a "reliable informant" need not be disclosed by the police; *Terry* v. *Ohio*, 392 U.S. 1 (1968), supporting the right of the police to stop and frisk a suspect as a means of self-protection. The Court sanctioned eavesdropping devices prior to the Omnibus Crime Act in *Osborn* v. *U.S.* 385 U.S. 323 (1966), saying it was permitted where the "commission of a specific offense" was charged, its use was "under the most precise and discriminating circumstances," and the effective administration of justice in a federal court was at stake. See also, *Michigan Law Review* 47 (December 1968): 265.

decade of opposition to the U.S. Supreme Court because of decisions involving the accused, but it also was nurtured by decisions which infuriated those in some regions where the "activist" Warren Court had endangered some long-standing patterns of life, especially in the Old South.

II

Mallory

———◆———

It is not new or novel to have strong and persistent criticisms directed toward the Supreme Court of the United States. It has been that way almost from the beginning of our constitutional system. Chief Justice John Marshall's celebrated opinion[1] of one hundred fifty years ago evoked hostility toward him and the Court which did not subside until his death sixteen years later. Chief Justice Roger B. Taney's effort for equilibrium in the federal system was not very well received by many in decisions of his day.

In the modern period, one hundred years after Marshall's. Court was remade several times by successive appointments, the nation was embroiled in controversy about the place of the judicial power in the American system when President Franklin D. Roosevelt, fresh from a strong mandate of both popular and electoral vote, almost took the Court to a proverbial "cleaning" with his court-packing plan of 1937. More recently, of course, the Warren Court was under almost continuous attack following decisions of most of its sixteen years.

Among the decisions of the Warren Court only a few stand out as having provoked strong and sometimes acrimonious attacks from among influential members of the Congress, candidates for the presidency, great numbers of justices of the highest courts of the states, countless other public officials

1. *McCulloch* v. *Maryland*, 4 Wheat. 316 (1819).

(national, state, and local), and a generous mixture of private citizens.

In one of his last opinions, Chief Justice Warren gave the decision in *Powell* v. *McCormick*, involving the power of the House of Representatives to exclude Adam Clayton Powell.[2] He cited with approval an 1881 case on the power of any branch of the government:

> Especially is it competent and proper for this court to consider whether its [the legislature's] proceedings are in conformity with the Constitution and laws, because, living under a written constitution, no branch or department of the government is supreme; and it is the province and duty of the judicial department to determine in cases regularly brought before them, whether the power of any branch of the government, and even those of the legislature in the enactment of laws, have been exercised in conformity to the Constitution; and if they have not, to treat their acts as null and void.

In that opinion Justice Samuel F. Miller was affirming what Alexander Hamilton had written in *The Federalist* No. 78:

> The interpretation of the laws is the proper and peculiar province of the courts. A constitution is, in fact, and must be regarded by the judges, as a fundamental law. It therefore belongs to them to ascertain its meaning, as well as the meaning of any particular act proceeding from the legislative body . . . the Constitution ought to be preferred to the statute, the intention of the people to the intention of their agents. . . . They [judges] ought to regulate their decisions by the fundamental laws, rather than by those which are not fundamental.

Hamilton was talking about the power of the judiciary to review acts of legislative bodies, but also about the supremacy of the Constitution. Furthermore, a part of the " peculiar province of the courts " is the place of the U.S. Supreme Court as a court of last resort where issues are presented involving

2. Decided June 16, 1969. The case cited was *Kilbourn* v. *Thompson*, 103 U.S. 168, 169.

constitutional questions and cases finally decided. They are not final in an absolute sense, to be sure, for subsequent decisions may modify earlier ones and even reverse them. Otherwise, decisions can be overruled when replacements are made on the court with appointed successors with different views, or by constitutional amendment.[3]

Our juridical system is an adversary system and the courts must ultimately decide cases between adversaries. It follows that because of the nature of some controversies which involve constitutional questions the loser not only will experience keen disappointment, but may demonstrate resistance and even vigorous opposition for a long time to decisions favorable to the other side. Some of these decisions where feeling is high will affect only a small, if vocal, minority. Other decisions will be regional, such as the segregation cases. Still others will be nearly nationwide, such as some of the national security cases.

Among the decisions of the Warren Court few equal the continuing and sometimes widespread opposition to those outlawing prayers in classrooms, those relating to interrogations and confessions, and those concerning the accused's right to counsel. Still, these same decisions evoked widespread praise and support from libertarians as extending human rights and liberties and protecting persons in the clutches of the law from unfair practices. Taken singly, decisions such as these might not have produced more than a temporary clamor against the U.S. Supreme Court, but they were both preceded and accompanied by decisions in some controversial national security cases.

This was especially true with the decisions in *Jencks, Watkins,* and *Sweezy,* all decided in 1957.[4] These decisions were viewed by supporters of the late Senator Joseph McCarthy as being "soft" on communism and intensified animosity toward the Supreme Court and particularly Chief Justice Earl Warren.

3. A decision might indicate that a change in legislation could produce different results.
4. *Jencks* v. *U.S.,* 353 U.S. 657; *Watkins* v. *U.S.,* 354 U.S. 178; *Sweezy* v. *N. H.,* 354 U.S. 234.

Clinton E. Jencks had been convicted of falsely stating he was not a member of the Communist party or affiliated with it. The main testimony against him was by two informants for the FBI. During the trial, Jencks attempted to obtain access to the testimony as part of his defense, but this was denied. With only Justice Tom C. Clark dissenting, the Court held that Jencks was entitled to inspect all the reports the FBI had about the case, "written and, orally made, as recorded by the F.B.I., touching the events and activities as to which they testified at the trial." It further held that Jencks could decide whether they would be of help in his case or not, for "only the defense is adequately equipped to determine the effective use . . . and thereby furthering the accused's defense . . . . Justice requires no less." Having the trial judge inspect the reports and making that determination was disapproved.

While those involved in national security cases were assessing the effect of the Jencks decision, the Court two weeks later announced decisions in *Watkins* and *Sweezy*.

John T. Watkins was convicted of violating a provision of the U.S. Code making it a misdemeanor for an individual summoned as a witness by either house of the Congress or any committee of either house to refuse to answer questions "pertinent" to the inquiry. He was summoned to testify before the subcommittee of the House of Representatives Committee on Un-American Activities. He testified freely about his own activities and associations but he refused to answer questions about other persons and to verify whether they had been members of the Communist party. He based his refusal on the view that the questions put to him about others were outside the authority of the committee and not relevant to its work.

In its opinion, the Supreme Court gave detailed consideration to the investigatory powers of legislative bodies. Chief Warren delivered the opinion of the Court, with only Justice Clark dissenting:

The power of the Congress to conduct investigations is inherent in the legislative process. That power is broad. It encompasses inquiries concerning the administration of existing laws as well as proposed or possibly needed statutes. It includes surveys of defects in our . . . system. It comprehends probes into departments. . . . But, broad as is this power of inquiry, it is not unlimited. There is no general authority to expose the private affairs of individuals without justification in terms of the functions of the Congress. . . . Nor is the Congress a law enforcement or trial agency.[5]

Warren then proceeded to restrict the congressional power of inquiry to the "legitimate" tasks of the Congress, saying that investigations could not be conducted for the personal "aggrandizement of the investigators" or to "punish" those being investigated. He hinted that the Court agreed with Watkins that the sole purpose of the inquiry was to bring public reaction against him for his past beliefs, expressions, and associations. He said that the power of the Congress to expose cannot be for "the sake of exposure." To do so would mean an invasion of the private rights of individuals.

What stirred up further wrath against the decision was the following:

Who can define the meaning of "un-American"? What is that single, solitary principle of the form of government as guaranteed by our "Constitution"? There is no need to dwell upon the language, however. At one time, perhaps, the resolution might have been read and narrowly to confine the Committee to the subject of propaganda. The events that have transpired in the fifteen years before the interrogation of petitioner makes such a construction impossible at this date.[6]

In circumscribing these investigations often criticized as freewheeling, Warren concluded that their decision would not prevent the Congress, through its committees, "from obtaining any information needed for the proper fulfillment of its role in our scheme of government." All any committee needed

5. 354 U.S. 178, 187.
6. *Ibid.*, 202.

to do was observe the rights of individuals against illegal encroachment.

The companion case of *Sweezy* resulted from investigations by the attorney general of New Hampshire on behalf of the legislature under its resolution directing him to determine whether there were "subversive" persons in the state and to recommend legislation on the subject.

Under inquiry by the attorney general, Paul M. Sweezy answered most of the questions, including whether he was a Communist, but he would not answer questions relating to (1) the contents of a lecture he had delivered at the state university and (2) his knowledge of the Progressive party of the state or its members. He did not plead self-incrimination but rather that the questions were not pertinent to the inquiry and they violated his First Amendment rights.

As in the *Watkins* case, Chief Justice Warren delivered the opinion of the Court. There was no denial that the New Hampshire legislature could make the attorney general a one-man committee acting in its behalf. But the high court said that Sweezy was improperly questioned about his lecture and his right to associate with others.

> The essentiality of freedom in the community of American universities is almost self evident. No one should underestimate the vital role in a democracy that is played by those who guide and train our youth. To impose any strait jacket upon the intellectual leaders of our colleges and universities would imperil the future of the Nation. . . . Scholarship cannot flourish in an atmosphere of suspicion and distrust. Teachers and students must always remain free to inquire, to study and evaluate, to gain new maturity and understanding; otherwise our civilization will stagnate and die.[7]

The immediate reaction in the Congress was to attempt, by legislation, to withdraw prosecutions for contempt of Congress from the appellate jurisdiction of the Supreme Court, but these efforts failed.

7. 354 U.S. 234, 249.

On June 8, 1959, two more decisions were handed down involving national security problems. One was *Uphaus* v. *Wyman*, the other *Barenblatt* v. *U.S.*[8]

Uphaus brought New Hampshire back into the picture. Again as in *Sweezy*, the state's attorney general was a one-man investigating committee acting under a legislative resolution to determine whether there were subversive persons in the state. Willard Uphaus was asked to produce certain documents relating to a voluntary corporation incorporated under the laws of New Hampshire, known as the World Fellowship, Inc. It maintained a summer camp and the attorney general directed questions to Uphaus about his own activities, with which he complied. But he refused to produce a list of names of the camp's employees for two summer periods and the correspondence he had with persons who came to the camp as speakers. Neither would he produce the names of all persons who attended the camp. Uphaus claimed that since the Congress had occupied the field of subversive activities, the state of New Hampshire was without power to investigate in the same area.

The U.S. Supreme Court considered only the question of the validity of the order to produce the list of guests. Justice Clark in giving the opinion for a divided court (four dissents), distinguished the case from *Sweezy*, saying that the "academic and political freedoms . . . are not present here in the same degree, since World Fellowship is neither a university nor a political party. . . ." He also found that the state had the right to require the production of corporate papers of a "state-chartered corporation in an inquiry to determine whether corporate activity is violative of state policy. . . ." He concluded that the demand for the documents was a proper one, and "we do not impugn appellant's good faith in the assertion of what he believed to be his rights. But three courts have disagreed with him in interpreting those rights."[9]

The dissenting justices claimed that the state did not have

8. 360 U.S. 72; 360 U.S. 109.
9. 360 U.S. 72, 77, 82.

any proper legislative end in mind. To them there was no showing that was sufficient to "counterbalance the interest of privacy as it relates to freedom of speech and assembly." [10]

In the same volume of U.S. Reports, is the companion case of *Barenblatt* v. *U.S.*, with the same divided court.

In this case Lloyd Barenblatt was a teaching fellow and former student at the University of Michigan. He refused to answer questions put to him by the subcommittee of the House Committee on Un-American Activities (HUAC) during the course of its inquiry about alleged Communist infiltration into the field of education.

Justice John M. Harlan distinguished between issues in this case and *Sweezy* since both involved the field of education.

> We think that investigatory power in this domain is not to be denied, solely because the field of education is involved. Nothing in the prevailing opinions since *Sweezy* . . . stands for a contrary view. The vice existing there was the questioning of Sweezy, as to the contents of a lecture given at the University of New Hampshire, and his connection with the Progressive Party, then on the ballot as a normal political party in some 26 states. . . . This is a very different thing from inquiring into the extent to which the Communist Party has succeeded in infiltrating into our universities, or elsewhere. . . . The constitutional legislative power of Congress in this instance is beyond question. . . . We conclude that the balance between the individual and the governmental interests here at stake must be struck in favor of the latter, and that therefore the provisions of the First Amendment have not been offended. [11]

Those who applauded the decisions in *Watkins* and *Sweezy* were dumbfounded with the *Uphaus* and *Barenblatt* decisions. These latter appeared to tell the Congress that it could proceed with HUAC type investigations. C. Herman Pritchett has criticized the decision in *Barenblatt* saying that "again" the court "fumbled an opportunity to develop a theory of judicial control which in practice would take into account of the need

10. *Ibid.*, 107, 108.
11. 360 U.S. 109, 129, 133, 134.

to safeguard both legislative rights to decide what information is needed and private rights against coercion and humiliation." [12] He also mentioned the need to separate the legislative power to investigate and the power to compel testimony, stating that the latter should be more narrowly prescribed.

To some, these modifications by *Uphaus* and *Barenblatt* of *Watkins* and *Sweezy* were the result of some major rethinking by the Court, while others believed that the Court was very sensitive to the criticism they had received in a brief span of five years. In any event spirited opposition to the Court in these situations gradually subsided.

One week after the decisions in *Sweezy* and *Watkins*, on June 24, 1957, the Court gave its decision in *Mallory* v. *U.S.*[13] This decision extended protection to an accused from unnecessary delay in arraignment and had the effect of denying enforcement officers an opportunity to extract confessions prior to arraignment.

The critics of this decision were unrelenting. Ten years afterward it was characterized by the U.S. district judge for the District of Columbia, Alexander Holtzoff, as "one of the contributing causes to the difficulty in enforcing the criminal law and in the increasing rate of crime." Of the doctrine expressed in the decision, he said it was "predicated not on any constitutional principle, but merely is a procedural matter." [14] It was, in fact, based on a "rule" of procedure.

The facts in *Mallory* are as follows. Andrew R. Mallory was convicted in the Federal District Court for the District of Columbia for the crime of rape and was sentenced to death. The rape occurred at 6:00 P.M. on April 7, 1954, in an apartment house basement. The victim had descended into the basement to do laundry, but experiencing some problem with detaching a hose, she sought help from the janitor who

12. C. Herman Pritchett, *Congress Versus the Supreme Court 1957– 1960* (Minneapolis: University of Minnesota Press, 1961). Pritchett has several chapters clearly analyzing national security cases and related issues.

13. 354 U.S. 449.

14. Senate Subcommittee *Hearings*, 1967, p. 261.

lived in a basement apartment with his wife, two grown sons, a young son, and Mallory, a nineteen-year-old half brother. Mallory was alone in the apartment at the time but assisted the victim in detaching the hose and then he returned to his apartment. Shortly thereafter a masked man whose general features were identified to resemble Mallory's and his two grown nephews attacked the woman. The three then disappeared from the apartment house. Mallory was apprehended the following afternoon between 2:00 and 2:30 P.M. and was taken along with his older nephews, also suspects, to police headquarters. At least four officers questioned him there in the presence of other officers for thirty to forty-five minutes, and began the inquiry by telling him his brother said he, Mallory, was the assailant. This he denied. About 4:00 P.M. the three were asked and agreed to take a lie detector test. It was two hours later before the officer in charge of the polygraph machine could be located. The nephews were questioned first, and it was about 8:00 P.M. when the polygraph operator and Mallory went into a small room for the test. About an hour and one-half of steady interrogation followed and Mallory said that "he could have done this crime, or that he might have done it." He finally said he was responsible. At about 10:00 P.M. after he had repeated his confession to other officers an effort was made to reach a U.S. commissioner for purpose of arraignment. One was not available at the time; so the officers obtained Mallory's consent to take a physical examination by the deputy coroner who reported no indicia of physical or psychological coercion by the police in their interrogation during the prior eight hours, approximately.

Next, Mallory was confronted by the complaining witness and practically "every man in the Sex squad." In the presence of three officers, he repeated his confession. Between 11:30 P.M. and 12:30 A.M. he dictated the confession to a typist. The next morning he was brought before a commissioner.

His trial was delayed about a year because there was some doubt that he had the capacity to understand the proceedings against him, but his confession was introduced in evidence.

Justice Felix Frankfurter's opinion, following appeal to the

U.S. Supreme Court said that "the case calls for the proper application of Rule 5 (a) of the Federal Rules of Criminal Procedure." That rule provided for appearances before a magistrate.

> An officer making an arrest under a warrant issued upon a complaint or any person making an arrest without a warrant shall take the arrested person without unnecessary delay before the nearest available commissioner, before any other nearby officer empowered to commit persons charged with offenses against the laws of the United States. When a person arrested without a warrant is brought before a commissioner or other officer, a complaint shall be filed forthwith.[15]

Frankfurter observed that the duty of officers under the rule to arraign "without unnecessary delay" did not call for mechanical or automatic obedience. Circumstances could justify a brief delay between arrest and arraignment, as for instance, where the story volunteered by the accused is susceptible of quick verification through third parties. But the delay, he said, must not be of a nature to give opportunity for the extraction of a confession. He noted that Mallory was detained at police headquarters for another four hours after being asked to submit to the polygraph test, "during which arraignment could easily have been made in the same building." More than that, Frankfurter said:

> He was not told of his rights to counsel or to a preliminary examination before a magistrate, or was he warned that he might keep silent and that "any statement made by him may be used against him." . . . Not until he had confessed, when any judicial question had lost its purpose, did the police arraign him.

15. 354 U.S. 449, 451, 452. As brought out in the Senate hearings in 1967, ten years later, critics of the decision were quick to point out that the *Mallory* opinion was predicated on the rule, "not on any constitutional principle, but merely is a procedural matter. . . . Since this rule is not based on any constitutional principle, it can be changed by legislation." Senate Subcommittee *Hearings*, 1967, p. 260.

We cannot sanction this extended delay, resulting in confession, without subordinating the general rule of prompt arraignment to the discretion of arresting officers in finding exceptional circumstances for its disregard.[16]

Mallory was decided in 1957. During the next eight years efforts were made to get legislation passed which would have the effect of softening the decision, but it was not until 1966 that a bill passed and it was vetoed by the president. A similar bill was passed in 1967, affecting only the District of Columbia, and it was given executive approval.[17] But during the intervening decade the controversy over the *Mallory* decision (and the *Miranda* and *Wade* decisions) was continuous.

In August, 1958, the Conference of Chief Justices adopted a report of the Committee on Federal-State Relationships as affected by Judicial Decisions. It was a lengthy document. It ranged wide over concepts of the federal system, and reviewed the impact, as the state justices saw it, of major national legislative programs of the prior two decades or more. The major themes were about decisions of the U.S. Supreme Court, both as that court interpreted statutes, state and national, and as the Court interpreted constitutional provisions. Two statements are worth noting:

Second only to the increasing dominance of the national government has been the development of the immense power of the Supreme Court in both state and national affairs. It is not merely the final arbiter of the law; it is the maker of policy in many major social and economic fields. It is not subject to the restraints to which a legislative body is subject. There are points at which it is difficult to delineate precisely the line which should circumscribe the judicial function and separate it from that of policymaking. Thus, usually within narrow limits, a court may be called upon in the ordinary course of its duties to make what is actually a policy decision by choosing between two rules, either of which might be deemed applicable to the situation presented in a pending case.

16. 354 U.S. 455.
17. Public Law 90-226, 90th Congress, H.R. 10783 of December 27, 1967.

But if and when a court in construing and applying a constitutional provision or a statute becomes a policy maker, it may leave construction behind and exercise functions which are essentially legislative in character, whether they serve in practical effect as a constitutional amendment or as an amendment of a statute. It is here that we feel the greatest concern, and it is here that we think the greatest restraint is called for. There is nothing new in urging judicial self-restraint, though there may be, and we think there is, new need to urge it.

And in its "Conclusions" the report contained this statement:

It is strange, indeed, to reflect that under a constitution which provides for a system of checks and balances and of distribution of power between national and state governments one branch of one government—the Supreme Court—should attain the immense, and in many respects, dominant, power which it now wields.

The state justices also expressed concern in a host of other issues and specific decisions with which they disagreed, but the report was especially strong in its opposition to the decision in *Sweezy*.[18]

Six months after the state chief justices adopted their report another stinging criticism was made of the Supreme Court when the House of Delegates of the American Bar Association adopted its "Resolutions of the Special Committee on Communist Tactics, Strategy, and Objectives." It singled out the *Watkins* decision for special treatment, but in various statements it also called upon the Congress, both houses, to define more clearly their investigatory intentions and clarify their procedures "in writing of the precise terms of the basic authority" of committees and through legislation, if necessary, comply with the Supreme Court's decisions and still accomplish their investigative goals.

18. 354 U.S. 234. The justices supported the view of Justices Tom C. Clark and Harold H. Burton that the state's interest in self-preservation justified the intrusion into Sweezy's personal affairs.

Thus, in a few decisions, the U.S. Supreme Court induced unusually strong criticisms not only from the judicial family, but from many influential leaders in the Congress, law enforcement officials, and leaders of the American Bar Association. Newspaper editors also joined to make a substantial bloc of opposition to the direction of court decisions.

The build-up of this opposition to the Warren Court had been under way especially after May 17, 1954, when the court overruled *Plessy* v. *Ferguson* in *Brown* v. *Board of Education*, a decision intended to eliminate segregation in the schools.[19] Criticism, sometimes abusive, was to remain to the end of the Warren Court in 1969.

19. 163 U.S. 537 (1896); 347 U.S. 483 (1954).

III

Miranda and *Wade*

The desegregation cases and their aftermath irritated the Old South and many areas outside the South where *de facto* segregation continued to exist. Chief Justice Warren's requirement in *Brown* that segregation be eliminated in the "separate but equal schools" and with "all deliberate speed" had not ended segregation as means were found to delay it. Much of the bitter reaction toward the U.S. Supreme Court resulting from the national security cases and segregation cases would have gradually subsided had it not been for the *Mallory* case of 1957, just presented in chapter two, and the *Gideon, Escobedo, Miranda,* and *Wade* cases decided in a short span of four years.[1] These cases, plus rising crime rates and serious disturbances in many cities, set the stage for the Senate version of Title II of the omnibus crime bill.

On March 18, 1963, the U.S. Supreme Court gave its opinion in *Gideon* v. *Wainwright.*[2] The facts and circumstances can be briefly stated.

1. *Gideon* v. *Wainwright*, 372 U.S. 335 (1963); *Escobedo* v. *Illinois*, 378 U.S. 478 (1964); *Miranda* v. *Arizona*, 384 U.S. 436 (1966); *U.S.* v. *Wade*, 388 U.S. 218 (1967).

2. For an excellent presentation of phases of this case and related cases involving defendant's rights during the first decade of the Warren Court, see G. Theodore Mitau, *Decade of Decision—The Supreme Court and the Constitutional Revolution 1954–1964* (New York: Charles Scribner's Sons, 1967). One of the most important contributions in recent years on the subject of the defendant's rights, pub-

Clarence Earl Gideon was charged in a Florida court with having broken into and entered a pool room with an intent to commit a misdemeanor, a felony under Florida law. He appeared in court without funds, without a lawyer. He asked the court to appoint a lawyer for him, but this was refused. The following colloquy took place.

> THE COURT: Mr. Gideon, I am sorry, but I cannot appoint Counsel to represent you in this case. Under the laws of the State of Florida, the only time the Court can appoint Counsel to represent a Defendant is when that person is charged with a capital offense. I am sorry, but I will have to deny your request to appoint Counsel to defend you in this case.
> THE DEFENDANT: The United States Supreme Court says I am entitled to be represented by Counsel.[3]

The jury found him guilty. (He conducted his own defense.) The sentence was five years. He then attacked the conviction on the ground that lack of counsel denied him his fundamental rights. The Supreme Court of Florida rejected his contention. He then penciled a note to the U.S. Supreme Court requesting a review. That court granted certiorari and appointed Attorney Abe Fortas (later associate justice) to represent him.

The question was: Did the right to counsel in a state court prevail notwithstanding a Florida rule that counsel would be provided only in capital cases? At issue also was the decision fifteen years earlier in *Betts* v. *Brady*,[4] still controversial because of the opinion by Justice Owen J. Roberts which concluded with these words:

> As we have said, the Fourteenth Amendment prohibits the conviction and incarceration of one whose trial is offensive to the common and fundamental ideas of fairness and right, and while want of counsel in a particular case may

---

lished in 1958, is David Fellman, *The Defendant's Rights* (New York: Rinehart & Company).

3. 372 U.S. 335, 337.
4. 316 U.S. 455 (1942).

result in a conviction lacking in such fundamental fairness, *we cannot say that the amendment embodies an inexorable command that no trial for any offense, or in any court, can be fairly conducted and justice accorded a defendant who is not represented by counsel.*[5]

Justice Hugo L. Black, in the opinion for the Court in *Gideon*, held that the decision in *Betts* had departed from precedent and the judgment of the Court was to return to those precedents.

Not only these precedents but reason and reflection require us to recognize that in our adversary system of criminal justice, any person hailed into court, who is too poor to hire a lawyer, cannot be assured a fair trial unless counsel is provided for him. This seems to us to be an obvious truth. . . . "Left without the aid of counsel he may be put on trial without a proper charge, and convicted upon incompetent evidence, or evidence irrelevant to the issue or otherwise inadmissible. . . . He requires the guiding hand of counsel at every step in the proceedings against him. Without it, though he be not guilty, he faces the danger of conviction because he does not know how to establish his innocence."[6]

Justice Black's words gave proper comfort to the unfortunate Gideon and others, too, at that time, but also gave consternation and dismay to countless law enforcement officers, including trial judges. Gideon's successful challenge to the Florida system was given much publicity in and out of legal circles and the consequences of the decision were substantial. Appeals from at least a dozen states were remanded for retrial or dismissal, and one report has it that hundreds of prisoners were released in Florida alone as the result of the decision. On October 14, 1963, for example, the U.S. Supreme Court remanded to Florida a number of cases on the same

5. *Ibid.*, 473. (Emphasis supplied.)
6. 372 U.S. 335, 344, citing also *Powell* v. *Alabama*, 287 U.S. 45, 68–69 (1932).

grounds as *Gideon*.[7] Numerous legislatures and state courts, however, soon complied with the Court decision to make provision for counsel and to improve what already existed in like situations.

The next June, *Escobedo* was decided.[8] It, too, involved denial of access to counsel, the failure of the police to advise the accused of his right to remain silent during interrogation, and the use during trial of incriminating evidence obtained during such interrogation.

Danny Escobedo was questioned by the Chicago police on two different occasions after a shooting incident in January, 1960. In the course of the interrogation, Danny made an incriminating statement which implicated him in the murder plot. The assistant state's attorney later testified he did not advise Danny of his constitutional rights, nor did any other official. Justice Arthur J. Goldberg who gave the opinion for the U.S. Supreme Court after appeal from conviction got to the issue this way:

> It is argued that if the right to counsel is afforded prior to indictment, the number of confessions obtained by the police will diminish significantly, because most confessions are obtained during the period between arrest and indictment, and "any lawyer worth his salt will tell the suspect in no uncertain terms to make no statement to police under any circumstances." . . . This argument, of course, cuts two ways. The fact that many confessions are obtained during this period points up its critical nature as a "stage when legal aid and advice" are surely needed. . . . The right to counsel would indeed be hollow if it began at a period when few confessions were obtained. There is necessarily a direct relationship between the importance of a stage to the police in their quest for a confession and the criticalness of that stage to the accused in his need for legal advice. Our Constitution, unlike some others, strikes the balance in favor of the right of the

7. *Pickelsimer* v. *Wainwright*, 375 U.S. 2 (1963). Judgments in ten cases were vacated for further consideration in light of *Gideon*.
8. 378 U.S. 478 (1964).

accused to be advised by his lawyer of his privilege against self-incrimination.[9]

Goldberg was emphatic about *when* an accused should have his warnings and his right to counsel. The timing was important. He put it this way. When the investigation is "no longer a general inquiry into an unresolved crime but has begun to focus on a particular suspect . . . and its purpose is to elicit a confession" *then* the accused must have an opportunity to consult with an attorney.[10]

The decision had dissenters. They thought the majority went too far and the result would become an undue burden on the agencies for law enforcement. Justice Byron R. White was so critical of the majority view that he said he believed that police cars would have to carry public defenders with them. He also expressed concern that thereafter confessions would not be admissible whether given voluntarily or not. These views were used to great advantage by opponents of the majority position during the hearings on the crime bill in 1967 and especially during the Senate debate on Title II. White also had this to say:

> The decision is thus another major step in the direction of the goal which the Court seemingly has in mind—to bar from evidence all admissions obtained from an individual suspected of crime, whether involuntarily made or not. It does of course put us one step "ahead" of the English judges who have had the good sense to leave the matter of a discretionary one with the trial court. I reject this step and the invitation to go farther which the Court has not issued. . . . I do not suggest for a moment that law enforcement will be destroyed by the rule announced today. The need for peace and order is too insistent for that. *But it will be crippled and its task made a great deal more difficult, all in my opinion, for unsound, unstated reasons, which can find no home in any provisions of the Constitution.*[11]

9. *Ibid.*, 488.
10. *Ibid.*, 490, 491.
11. *Ibid.*, 495, 496, 499. (Emphasis supplied.)

Two years after the *Escobedo* decision, on June 13, 1966, the Supreme Court gave its decision in *Miranda* v. *Arizona*,[12] regarded by many as the most controversial decision in many years because it affected criminal law enforcement and the rights of the accused. Chief Justice Warren wrote the opinion for the majority, but as in *Escobedo* there were four dissenters: Justices Clark, Harlan, White, and Stewart. The facts in *Miranda* are as follows.

On March 3, 1963, an eighteen-year-old girl was kidnapped and forcibly raped near Phoenix, Arizona. On the morning of March 13, 1963, Ernesto Miranda was arrested and taken to a police station. Ernesto was twenty-three years of age, indigent, with formal education ceasing upon completion of half of the ninth grade. A doctor who later testified examined him and reported that he was of the schizophrenic type, but that he was "alert and oriented as to time, place and person" and intelligent within normal limits, competent to stand trial, and sane within the legal definition.

At a police station line-up, the victim identified him as the one who had attacked her. He was then taken into a separate room where two officers began interrogating him at about 11:30 A.M. Ernesto at first denied his guilt, but within a short time he gave a detailed oral confession and then wrote out and signed a brief statement admitting and describing the crime. This was accomplished in about two hours without any force, threats, or promises. There is no evidence that he was given any warnings about his rights.[13]

He was tried and convicted. An appeal later reached the U.S. Supreme Court. From his opinion, it is apparent that the chief justice acknowledged the adverse reactions of the decision in *Escobedo*. He wrote a discourse on the place of the accused in society, the restraints that society places on its members who violate its precepts, the commonly accepted methods of law enforcement, and the rights of an accused. He said in part:

12. 384 U.S. 436.
13. *Ibid.*, 518.

We start here, as we did in *Escobedo*, with the premise that our holding is not an innovation in our jurisprudence, but is an application of principles long recognized and applied in other settings. We have undertaken a thorough re-examination of the *Escobedo* decision and the principles it announced, and we reaffirm it. That case was but an explication of basic rights that are enshrined in our Constitution.[14]

Warren also evaluated prior related cases, concepts, and doctrines presumably to sufficiently fortify his position in the anticipation of a torrent of opposition. Even though he said the Court reaffirmed the decision in *Escobedo*, he sought to clarify that decision so narrowly decided, to assist in the determination of acceptable standards which law enforcement officials could safely follow. If the "old ways" of obtaining confessions were out, what would take their place?

> To summarize, we hold that when an individual is taken into custody or otherwise deprived of his freedom by the authorities in any significant way and is subjected to questioning, the privilege against self-incrimination is jeopardized. Procedural safeguards must be employed to protect the privilege, unless other effective means are adopted to notify the person of his right of silence and to assure that the exercise of the right will be scrupulously honored, the following measures are required. He must be warned prior to any questioning that he has the right to remain silent, that anything he says can be used against him in a court of law, that he has the right to the presence of an attorney, and that if he cannot afford an attorney one will be appointed for him prior to any questioning if he so desires. Opportunity to exercise the rights must be afforded to him throughout the interrogation. After such warnings have been given, and such opportunity afforded him, the individual may knowingly and intelligently waive these rights and agree to answer questions or make a statement. But unless and until such warnings and waiver are demonstrated by the prosecution at trial, no evidence obtained as a result of interrogation can be used against him.[15]

14. *Ibid.*, 442.
15. *Ibid.*, 478, 479.

Critics of the Warren opinion said that by a single opinion and only by a majority of one "time-honored" procedures were cast aside. Justice Harlan was cryptic in his dissent.

I believe the decision of the Court represents poor constitutional law and entails harmful consequences for the country at large. How serious these consequences may prove to be only time can tell. . . . To incorporate this notion into the Constitution requires a strained reading of history and precedent.[16]

Warren's answer is contained in these words:

A recurrent argument made in these cases is that society's need for interrogation outweighs the privilege. This argument is not unfamiliar to this Court. . . . The whole thrust of our foregoing discussion demonstrates that the Constitution has prescribed the rights of the individual when confronted with the power of government when it provided in the Fifth Amendment that an individual cannot be compelled to be a witness against himself.[17]

Warren undoubtedly recalled Justice White's comment in *Escobedo* that public defenders would need to be in every police car, for he said:

This does not mean, as some have suggested, that each police station must have a "station house lawyer" present at all times to advise prisoners. It does mean, however, that if police propose to interrogate a person they must make known to him that he is entitled to a lawyer and that if he cannot afford one, a lawyer will be provided for him prior to any interrogation.[18]

The chief justice's lengthy opinion endeavored to answer all arguments against prior related decisions and the prospects of an outcry against the decision in *Miranda*. He was aware also that the details just recited might appear inadequate to enforcement officers and trial judges. And if he might have

16. *Ibid.*, 504, 505.
17. *Ibid.*, 479.
18. *Ibid.*, 474.

regretted his "with all deliberate speed" phrase in the *Brown* desegregation case, one may well wonder whether there might also have been regret in the statement in *Miranda*:

> It is impossible for us to foresee the potential alternatives for protecting the privilege which might be devised by Congress or the States in the exercise of their creative rule-making capacities. Therefore we cannot say that the Constitution necessarily requires adherence to any particular solution for the inherent compulsions of the interrogation process as it is presently conducted. Our decision in no way creates a constitutional strait-jacket which will handicap sound efforts at reform, nor is it intended to have this effect. *We encourage Congress and the States to continue their laudable search for increasingly effective ways of protecting the rights of the individual while promoting efficient enforcement of our criminal laws.*[19]

In passing the omnibus crime bill two years later, the Congress accepted the chief justice's invitation for the Congress "to continue their laudable search for increasingly effective ways" of improving law enforcement. During the 1967 hearings and also during the debate in the Senate the question was raised frequently whether Title II of the crime bill was protecting the rights of the individual.

Almost exactly a year after *Miranda* came *Wade*.[20] It was the third major case which was the object of bitter opposition. It, too, was considered by its opponents as having struck a harmful blow at a nationwide effort to control crime. In *Wade*, the majority opinion held that an in-court identification of a suspect by an eyewitness was inadmissible under certain conditions.

On September 21, 1964, the federally insured bank at Eustace, Texas, was robbed. A man with a small strip of tape on each side of his face entered the bank, pointed a pistol at the cashier and the vice-president, the only persons in the bank at the time, and forced them to fill a pillow case with the bank's money. The man then drove away with an accomplice

19. *Ibid.*, 467. (Emphasis supplied.)
20. 388 U.S. 218 (1967).

who had been waiting in a stolen car outside the bank building. On March 23, 1965, an indictment was returned against Billy Joe Wade, and two others, for conspiring to rob the bank, and Wade and the accomplice for the robbery itself. Wade was arrested soon thereafter and counsel was appointed to represent him about three weeks later. On April 26, an FBI agent arranged, without notice to Wade's attorney, to have the two bank employees observe a line-up of Wade and some other prisoners in the courtroom of the local county courthouse. Each person in the line-up wore strips of tape as presumably worn by the robber. Each person in the line was asked to say something like "put the money in the bag"—the words allegedly used by the robber. Both bank employees identified Wade as the robber. They later identified him in the courtroom at the trial.

An appeal followed conviction and as in *Escobedo* and *Miranda*, the U.S. Supreme Court was divided. Justice William J. Brennan, Jr., gave the majority opinion.

Brennan made short work of Wade's objection that the line-up violated his privilege of self-incrimination. He said that "neither the lineup itself nor anything shown by this record that Wade was required to do in the lineup violated his privilege against self-incrimination." To exhibit his person for observation by a prosecution witness prior to his trial involved no compulsion to give evidence having "testimonial significance," nor was compelling him to speak within hearing distance of the witness or utter words used by the robber of a testimonial nature. He did not disclose any knowledge he might have about the robbery by this procedure. He was "required to use his voice as an identifying physical characteristic, not to speak his guilt." [21]

But if the procedure in the line-up did not violate Wade's rights, what about the event which did violate them?

In this case it is urged that the assistance of counsel at the lineup was indispensable to protect Wade's most basic

21. *Ibid.*, 222, 223.

right as a criminal defendant—his right to a fair trial in which the witnesses against him might be meaningfully cross-examined.[22]

What troubled the majority was that the prosecution considered the line-up as a "mere preparatory step" in putting together necessary evidence for its case, as it did in taking his fingerprints, analyzing a blood sample, and the like. Justice Brennan said there were differences. Taking the prints, blood sample, analyzing them and also some of his clothing, and his hair were "not critical stages since there is a minimal risk that his counsel's absence at such stages might derogate from his right to a fair trial." It was quite another matter, said Brennan, to have a confrontation with the witnesses and the accused. Under those conditions there is the chance "of innumerable dangers and variable factors which might seriously" derogate from a fair trial.[23]

Wade was decided by a divided Court. In his dissent, Justice White, joined by Justices Harlan and Potter Stewart, strongly objected to the right to counsel in a line-up.

> It matters not how well the witness knows the suspect, whether the witness is the suspect's mother, brother, or long-time associate, and no matter how long or well the witness observed the perpetrator at the scene of the crime. . . . The premise for the Court's rule is not the general unreliability of eyewitness identifications nor the difficulties inherent in observation, recall, and recognition. The Court assumes a narrower evil as the basis for its rule— improper police suggestion which contributes to erroneous identifications. The Court apparently believes that improper police procedures are so widespread that a broad prophylactic rule must be laid down, requiring the presence of counsel at all pretrial identifications, in order to detect recurring instances of police misconduct.[24]

The dissenting opinion also observed that in another case, decided that same day, *Stovall* v. *Denno*, a special line-up in a

22. *Ibid.*, 223.
23. *Ibid.*, 228.
24. *Ibid.*, 251, 252.

hospital room arranged by the police where the defendant did not have the benefit of counsel was approved, and although not emphasized, the line-up had but one Negro and he was identified by the victim as her assailant.[25]

Although the majority decisions in the above cases were pinpointed for "correction" by the Senate version of Title II of the crime bill, several related cases decided in 1967 made it clear that *Escobedo*, *Miranda*, and *Wade* were not isolated decisions. Some of these cases require brief consideration.

In *Garrity* v. *New Jersey*, decided in January, 1967, the appellants were police officers in certain New Jersey boroughs.[26] They were involved as a result of an investigation concerning the alleged fixing of traffic tickets. Each defendant was questioned, but before interrogation each was warned that anything said might be used against him in any criminal proceeding, that he had the privilege of refusing to answer if the disclosure would tend to be incriminating, but further that if they refused to answer they would be subject to removal from office. They responded, but over the objection. Some of the answers were used in subsequent prosecutions for conspiracy to obstruct the administration of the traffic laws of the state.

Justice William O. Douglas observed that the police officers had the choice "between self-incrimination or job forfeiture. . . . The option to lose their means of livelihood or to pay the penalty of self-incrimination is the antithesis of free choice to speak out or to remain silent." He concluded that "policemen, like teachers and lawyers, are not relegated to a watered-down version of constitutional rights."[27]

The following Monday, January 23, 1967, the Court gave its decision in *Sims* v. *Georgia*.[28] Isaac Sims, Jr., was convicted in superior court for the crime of rape. His conviction was affirmed by the state supreme court.

25. 388 U.S. 293 (1967).
26. 385 U.S. 493.
27. *Ibid.*, 496, 497, 500. Douglas also said that "where the choice is 'between the rock and the whirlpool' duress is inherent in deciding to 'waive' one or the other." *Ibid.*, 498.
28. 385 U.S. 538.

Sims, a Negro, was charged with raping a white woman and had been given the death penalty. On April 13, 1963, a twenty-nine-year-old white woman was driving home alone in her automobile when Sims drove up behind her in his car and forced her off the road. He then took the woman from her car into the nearby woods and forcibly raped her. He then returned to his car, but not being able to start it, he left on foot. Later he was apprehended by some Negro workers who had been alerted to be on the watch for him. He was then turned over to two state patrolmen.

The patrolmen took Sims to the office of a Dr. Jackson where his clothing was removed for testing for blood stains. Sims testified at his trial that while in Jackson's office he was knocked down, kicked over the right eye, and "pulled around the floor by his private parts." After four stitches were taken in his forehead, the patrolmen took him some thirty miles to the county jail. During the evening he saw a deputy sheriff he had known several years and agreed to make a statement. He signed a written confession in the presence of the sheriff and others.

At the trial, Sims testified to the abuse he had received while in Dr. Jackson's office. There was no contradictory statement to Sims's story except the doctor said he had not knocked Sims down. He made no mention of the other abuse. He did say that he was not in his office all the time that Sims was there.

Sims was convicted and he appealed. Justice Clark, giving the majority opinion, disagreed with the lower court and the state supreme court which had upheld the conviction. "There was a definite, clear-cut issue here. Petitioner testified that Doctor Jackson physically abused him while he was in his office and that he was suffering from that abuse when he made the statement, thereby rendering his confession involuntary and the result of coercion." [29]

On the fourth Monday in April, 1967, a unanimous Court decided *Clewis* v. *Texas*.[30] Marvin Peterson Clewis was con-

29. *Ibid.*, 543.
30. 386 U.S. 707.

victed of murder by having strangled his wife. A jury found him guilty and sentenced him to twenty-five years in prison. During the trial he tried to exclude evidence of three statements he made while in police custody. He claimed they had not been made voluntarily. But he was unsuccessful. (He had claimed he was subjected to physical assaults, but the high court did not go into the matter.)

The facts are these. Clewis was taken into custody about 6:00 A.M. on Sunday, July 8, 1962, and gave the police a statement late the following afternoon. Thereafter he was taken before a magistrate. He was subsequently tried and convicted, then appealed.

Justice Fortas, giving the opinion for the Supreme Court, said that "on a view most favorable to the state, petitioner had been held some 38 hours before being taken before a magistrate to be charged, had had very little sleep and very little food, and appeared to the police to be sick."[31] He had no contact with a lawyer. He had consistently denied all knowledge about his wife's death until he agreed to give a statement, confess to the crime, but confessing in a way, Fortas said, which was not consistent with the facts.

Then he gave another statement on Thursday, having had intermittent questioning. Still there was no counsel available to him.[32] During this time he was driven on a round trip of about six hundred miles, was given several "lie detector" tests, and detained in at least three police buildings. On July 13 he was delivered to the custody of the Midland County sheriff where he remained the next four days in jail. Still no lawyer. About 9:30 A.M. on Tuesday, July 17, he was again interrogated and this time by two deputy sheriffs. He began by denying his guilt. No lawyer was present and he had not been advised of his right to have one appointed. Afterward the

31. *Ibid.*, 709.
32. In a footnote, Fortas said that the state contended Clewis did consult with an attorney on Thursday morning, but Clewis said it was Friday morning. In any event, "the state does not dispute his testimony that the only subject discussed with the lawyer was the matter of a fee, and that the lawyer declined to represent him." *Ibid.*

district attorney arrived and Clewis confessed for the third time. He was not advised of his right to remain silent. About 10:45 A.M. preparation of a written statement was begun, following a formal warning of the right not to make it. But he signed the statement later used at the trial. Fortas said:

> We cannot hold that the petitioner's third statement was voluntary. . . . There was no break in the stream of events from the time Sunday morning . . . to the time Tuesday morning nine days later that he signed the statement in issue, sufficient to insulate the statement from the effect of all that went before.[33]

On October 23, 1967, the Supreme Court gave its decision in *Beecher* v. *Alabama*.[34] On June 15, 1965, Johnny Daniel Beecher escaped from the prison road gang in Camp Scottsboro, Alabama. The next day a woman's lifeless body was found about a mile from the camp. The following day Beecher was captured in Tennessee.

Tennessee police officers saw Beecher as he fled in an open field and fired a bullet into his right leg. He fell, and the local chief of police pressed a loaded gun to his face while another officer pointed a rifle against the side of his head. He was asked whether he had killed the woman. Denying it, he was called a liar and the chief said, "If you don't tell the truth I am going to kill you." The other officer then fired his rifle next to Beecher's ear and he then confessed. By June 23, the wounded leg—which was later amputated—had become so swollen and painful that he required morphine every four hours. Under this condition he signed the confession which had been prepared for him.[35]

The Supreme Court, *per curiam*, dealt briefly with the question of a voluntary confession, saying, "Even if we accept as accurate the state's version of what transpired there, the uncontradicted facts set forth above lead to the inescapable

33. *Ibid.*, 710.
34. 389 U.S. 35.
35. *Ibid.*, 36, 37.

conclusion that the petitioner's confessions were involuntary." [36]
One further illustration situation which helped put Title II
—Senate version—of the crime bill on its way to Senate debate
was the case of *Mempa* v. *Rhay*, decided on November 13,
1967.[37]
In a unanimous decision, Justice Thurgood Marshall gave
the opinion of the U.S. Supreme Court. Jerry Douglas Rhay,
seventeen years old, pleaded guilty to the offense of "joy-
riding," a plea given on the advice of a court-appointed
attorney. The judge placed him on probation for two years.
About four months later, however, the prosecutor moved to
have the probation revoked because Rhay was alleged to have
been involved in a burglary. He acknowledged the involve-
ment and was sentenced to ten years in prison. He did not
have counsel. The judge stated at the sentencing that he would
recommend to the parole board that Rhay serve only one
year. Six years later Rhay sought a writ of habeas corpus on
the ground that he was denied the right to counsel at the time
of the revocation hearing.
Marshall's commentary went as follows:

> Even more important in a case such as this is the fact that
> certain legal rights may be lost if not exercised at this
> stage. For one, Washington law provides that an appeal
> in a case involving a plea of guilty followed by probation
> can only be taken after sentence is imposed following
> revocation of probation. Therefore in a case where an
> accused agreed to plead guilty, although he had a valid
> defense, because he was offered probation, absence of
> counsel at the imposition of the deferred sentence might
> well result in loss of the right to appeal. . . . Without
> undertaking to catalog the various situations in which a
> lawyer could be of substantial assistance to a defendant
> in such a case, it can be reiterated that a plea of guilty
> might well be improperly obtained by the promise to have
> the defendant placed on the very probation the revocation
> of which furnished the occasion for desiring to withdraw
> the plea. An uncounseled defendant might very likely be

36. *Ibid.*, 38.
37. 389 U.S. 128.

unaware of this opportunity. . . . All we decide here is that a lawyer must be afforded at the proceeding whether it be labeled a revocation of probation or a deferred sentence.[38]

News reports about these and other decisions, together with many newspaper editorials which tied the rising crime rates with court "leniency," apparently made it easy for Senator McClellan to say during the Senate debate on the crime bill on May 1, 1968, that U.S. Supreme Court—and some federal appellate court—decisions, especially *Mallory, Escobedo,* and *Miranda* "are deplorable and demoralizing." He further said:

> They have weakened intolerably the force and effect of our criminal laws, and Congress had better do something about it. These decisions have set free many dangerous criminals and are daily preventing the conviction of others who are guilty. How can the freeing of known, admitted, and confessed murderers, robbers, and rapists by the courts, not on the basis of innocence but rather on the pretext of some alleged, minor, or dubious technicality, be justified.[39]

This was the mood of many in the Congress, especially in the Senate, and elsewhere, a mood strong enough to gain enough support by June, 1968, to pass a law, one title of which was deliberately and openly intended to "correct" the U.S. Supreme Court.

38. *Ibid.*, 135, 136, 137.
39. *Cong. Record*, 90th Cong., 2nd sess., 11201.

IV

Prelude to Law Making

THE CRIME COMMISSION

The Warren Court decisions just presented were widely recognized by many as making substantial changes in procedures designed to guarantee stricter observance of civil liberties. They were heralded by civil rights groups, but by upsetting some long-standing practices, opponents charged that the Supreme Court was an activist group and was bent on amending the Constitution by their pronouncements, or at least was legislating through judicial decisions.

During the late 1950s and into the 1960s unrest in many areas began to mount, especially in cities where nonwhite population concentrations were located. Charges of (and evidence of) discrimination in housing, employment, education, transportation, access to public facilities, and the like no doubt produced or helped produce violence and disorder. Crimes against the person and against property increased. Civil rights spokesmen, particularly in the black community, urged demonstrations, protest marches, sit-ins, and other forms of nonviolent action including disruptive tactics, to gain the nation's attention to the conditions of their lives. Other groups were more militant and even violent, respecting neither person, property, or process. The vast majority of these groups did not want injury to others or destruction of property, but rather to have their plight exposed so that it might somehow be remedied. In the process, however, confrontations resulted in countermeasures and brought injury and death. Willful destruction of property was frequent and evidence abounds that these events were not all one-sided.

Unquestionably these and related events brought the theme of "law and order" into the national political arena, focusing attention probably for the first time in such scope and magnitude of national concern on what had been traditionally a responsibility of the state and local governments: the preservation of the public peace, local order, and the protection of person and property. The solutions to the problems which gave impetus to the law and order theme were often submerged in face of widespread concern throughout the nation that there was a plague about and it had to be stopped. The disease was crime and criminals more than the *causes* of crime.[1]

Events in 1964 gave added national attention to the internal unrest. There was a substantial rise in crimes of violence. There was alarm that it was no longer safe to be on the public streets in many cities of the country.

Speaking before the Republican National Convention in July, 1964, President Dwight D. Eisenhower referred to those who roamed the streets seeking "helpless prey." One analysis is that prior to this comment there was no indication that "law and order" would be emphasized in the 1964 campaign. But prior to his acceptance speech, Senator Barry Goldwater said that he believed the abuse of law and order would be an issue and he would make it one.[2] He also indicated that the preservation of law and order was a national responsibility. He was quoted as saying that as president he would see that women

1. President Johnson in his address of July 27, 1967, said: "The only genuine, long-range solution for what has happened lies in an attack—mounted at every level—upon the conditions that breed despair and violence. All of us know what those conditions are: ignorance, discrimination, slums, poverty, disease, not enough jobs."

2. Richard H. Rovere, "Letter from San Francisco," *New Yorker*, July 25, 1964, p. 77. See also, Warren Lehman, "Crime, the Public, and the Crime Commission: A Critical Review of *The Challenge of Crime in a Free Society*, *Michigan Law Review* 66, no. 7 (May 1968): 1487–1540.

could go out on the streets with safety. With an already evident white "backlash" developing over the extension of civil rights by legislation and court decision, Goldwater had many sympathetic listeners. Although his foreign policy views are credited as a major reason for his defeat, he placed moral ·decay and crime ahead of his announced concerns about international affairs.

Among other views he urged that the Congress overrule the *Mallory* decision and that people be appointed to the courts who would favor the public and not the individual. And as if to avoid glaring inconsistency with his views on states' rights, he would "return" powers to the states so they could administer effectively the criminal law.[3]

Whether Goldwater's campaign emphasis or the totality of events within the country influenced him more, President Johnson sent a message to the Congress on March 8, 1965, announcing his plan to create a crime commission. He did not attack the Supreme Court, rather he urged that individual rights be protected. By executive Order No. 11236 of July 23, 1965, he created the Commission on Law Enforcement and Administration of Justice. The commission's report came eighteen months later in February, 1967.[4] It made more than two hundred specific recommendations "—concrete steps the Commission believes can lead to a safer and more just society."[5] Special task forces were formed to give special attention to organized crime, juvenile delinquency, narcotics

3. Richard H. Rovere, "A Reporter at Large," *New Yorker*, October 3, 1964, p. 206.
4. A Report by the President's Commission on Law Enforcement and Administration of Justice, *The Challenge of Crime in a Free Society* (Washington, D.C.: U.S. Government Printing Office, 1967); hereafter cited as President's Commission, *The Challenge of Crime*. Lehman, in "Crime, the Public, and the Crime Commission: A Critical Review of *The Challenge of Crime in a Free Society*," is very critical of the work of the commission.
5. President's Commission, *The Challenge of Crime*, p. v. In the summary these words appear: "But the recommendations are more than just a list of new procedures, new tactics, and new techniques. They are a call for a revolution in the way America thinks about crime."

and drug abuse, and drunkenness. Major emphasis was given
to police, courts, correction, and an assessment of the crime
problem in general.

In its chapter on "Crime in America," the commission
said:

> Each single crime is a response to a specific situation by a
> person with an infinitely complicated psychological and
> emotional makeup who is subject to infinitely complicated
> external pressures. Crime as a whole is millions of such
> responses. . . . There are some crimes so irrational, so
> unpredictable, so explosive, so resistant to analysis or
> explanation that they can no more be prevented or
> guarded against than earthquakes or tidal waves. . . . In
> a sense, social and economic conditions "cause" crime.
> Crime flourishes, and always had flourished, in city slums,
> those neighborhoods where overcrowding, economic
> deprivation, social disruption and racial discrimination
> are endemic. Crime flourishes in conditions of affluence,
> when there is much desire for material goods and many
> opportunities to acquire them illegally. Crime flourishes
> when there are many restless, relatively footloose young
> people in the population. Crime flourishes when standards
> of morality are changing rapidly.[6]

Our society cannot and will not accept an enlarged law-
lessness even if it must tolerate some of it. And even if it may
be at fault in tolerating many of the basic causes of crime, it
will not wait for long-range, time-consuming, money-con-
suming solutions to stop or reduce it. It will take the means at
hand to control it, even abusive means, in its concern and
belief that crime must be controlled and reduced, if not
wholly eliminated.

Of the defined crimes in which the Federal Bureau of
Investigation interests itself statistically on a national basis,
only a handful are ultimately collected and published in
Uniform Crime Reports. In any event, the submission of the data
are done voluntarily by the state and local agencies of government which participate. The crimes which adversely affect

6. *Ibid.*, pp. 17, 18.

personal safety are those of greatest concern to most Americans. These include willful homicide, forcible rape, aggravated assault, and robbery. *Uniform Crime Reports* for 1965 listed 357,894 crimes against the person. Additionally there were reported offenses of 1,173,201 cases of burglary, 762,352 of larceny ($50 and over), and 486,568 of motor vehicle thefts. The commission reported that although there were no data showing the percentage of aggravated assaults involving injury, the District of Columbia survey found that 84 percent involved personal injury. The data indicate that the likelihood of a serious personal attack in a given year is one in 550, but it is more likely to come not from strangers as it is from "spouses, family members, friends, or acquaintances."[7] This is an incredible commentary.

These and other data are but a partial story. No one knows how many crimes are unreported by victims, or how many more are known by the police or other authority but not reported at all. But reported or not, the data are alarming. The percentage change in the period 1960–67 was up 67 percent for aggravated assault, up 61 percent for forcible rape, up 88 percent for robbery, and up 34 percent for murder (mostly by handguns). Crimes of violence went up 73 percent, crimes against property up 91 percent, and larceny ($50 and over) up 107 percent. Auto thefts more than doubled![8]

It may be that some of these data reflect better gathering and reporting and that fewer crimes go unreported, but whether this is so or not, they are not comforting. These increases may well be caused by the existence of the many complex factors reported by the commission. It included a check list from *Uniform Crime Reports* statistics considered necessary to interpret otherwise bare statistical compilations.[9]

7. *Ibid.*, p. 19.

8. The commission counted some 2,800 federal crimes and a much larger number of state and local ones. It also observed that many crime rates vary significantly from place to place, but the crimes that concern Americans the most are those that affect their personal safety.

9. President's Commission, *The Challenge of Crime*, p. 27.

Density and size of the community population and the metropolitan area of which it is a part.

Composition of the population with reference particularly to age, sex, and race.

Economic status and mores of the population.

Relative stability of population, including commuters, seasonal, and other transient types.

Climate, including seasonal weather conditions.

Educational, recreational, and religious characteristics.

Effective strength of the police force.

Standards governing appointments to the police force.

Policies of the prosecuting officials and the courts.

Attitude of the public toward law enforcement problems.

The administrative and investigative efficiency of the local law enforcement agency.

One of the more disturbing items about the statistics is that of persons arrested in 1966–67 the largest group was under age twenty-five, and nearly half were under thirty. Even more disturbing is that of all arrested offenders, over 70 percent were under twenty-five when first arrested.[10]

The commission highlighted these shocking figures with an example of twenty-four hours of crimes reported in the District of Columbia.[11]

Friday, December 9:

9:15 A.M.	Strongarm robbery, street, $2.
10:15 A.M.	Armed robbery, liquor store, $1,500.
11:30 A.M.	Pocketbook snatched with force and violence, street, $3.
12:30 P.M.	Holdup with revolver, roofing company, $2,100.
2:40 P.M.	Holdup with gun, shoe store, $139.
3:20 P.M.	Holdup with gun, apartment, $92.
4:55 P.M.	Holdup with gun, bank, $8,716.
6:25 P.M.	Mugging, street, $5.
6:50 P.M.	Holdup with revolver, tourist home, $30.
7:00 P.M.	Strongarm robbery, street, $25.
7:05 P.M.	Holdup with gun, auto in parking lot, $61.
7:10 P.M.	Strongarm robbery, apartment house, $3.

10. *Ibid.*, p. 4.
11. *Ibid.*, p. 2.

7:15 P.M.	Holdup with revolver (employee shot twice), truck rental company, $200.
7:25 P.M.	Mugging, street, $5.
7:50 P.M.	Holdup with gun, transfer company, $1,400.
8:55 P.M.	Holdup with shotgun, newspaper substation, $100.
10:10 P.M.	Holdup with gun, hotel, $289.50.
10:15 P.M.	Strongarm robbery, street, $120.
10:30 P.M.	Holdup with gun, street, $59.50.
10:53 P.M.	Strongarm robbery, street, $175.
11:05 P.M.	Holdup, tavern, $40.
11:30 P.M.	Strongarm robbery, street, $3.
11:55 P.M.	Strongarm robbery, street, $175.

Saturday, December 10:

12:20 A.M.	Strongarm robbery, street, $19.
1:10 A.M.	Strongarm robbery, apartment house, $3.
3:25 A.M.	Strongarm robbery, street, $25.
3:50 A.M.	Holdup with knife, street, $23.
3:55 A.M.	Holdup with gun, street, $25.
4:20 A.M.	Robbery, with intent to rape, street, 75 cents.
6:25 A.M.	Holdup-rape, street, $20.
6:25 A.M.	Holdup with gun, tourist home, no amount listed.
6:45 A.M.	Holdup, street, $5.
7:30 A.M.	Holdup with knife, cleaners, $300.
7:40 A.M.	Strongarm robbery, street, $80.

Excluding the District of Columbia, most criminal acts are local in that they involve violations of *state* statutes. Obviously, the district serves in a similar capacity, but these acts are defined by the Congress. Thus, most offenses are the responsibility of state and local enforcement personnel and agencies. These represent as many as 40,000 police agencies in the nation. There are probably no accurate data on the total number of police in the United States, but it has been estimated that to bring these forces up to strength would require at least 50,000 more people than the "on board" count.[12]

12. Statement by Attorney General Ramsey Clark to the Subcommittee of the House of Representatives, March 15, 1967, House *Hearings*, 1967, p. 29.

Like most human organizations there are great deficiencies in the police systems of the nation. The commission reported the need for drastic improvement in all phases of the organization for the administration of justice in the United States. Its long list of recommendations attest to its findings about the causes of crime and recognize the complexity and difficulties of bringing about solutions.

One significant recommendation was for a program of federal support directed to eight major needs:

(1) State and local planning.
(2) Education and training of criminal justice personnel.
(3) Surveys and advisory agencies concerning the organization and operation of police departments, courts, prosecuting offices, and correction agencies.
(4) Development of a coordinated national information system for operational and research purposes.
(5) Funding of limited numbers of demonstration programs in agencies of justice.
(6) Scientific and technological research and development.
(7) Development of national and regional research centers.
(8) Grants-in-aid for operational innovations.[13]

The commission report was released on February 18, 1967. The president, of course, had knowledge of the recommendations earlier and they formed the basis for his reference to the problem of effective crime prevention and control in his State of the Union message of January 10, 1967, and his special message to the Congress of February 6, 1967.[14]

The president's emphasis was to improve local personnel and agencies involved in law enforcement and to relate them directly to the U.S. Department of Justice primarily through a system of grants direct to local units of government. In his 1966 message on crime he said:

Crime—the fact of crime and the fear of crime—marks the life of every American. We know its unrelenting pace:

13. President's Commission, *The Challenge of Crime*, p. xi.
14. In the February message he called for the enactment of the "Safe Streets and Crime Control Act of 1967."

A forcible rape every 26 minutes; a robbery every 5 minutes; an aggravated assault every 3 minutes; a car theft every minute; a burglary every 28 seconds. We know its cost in dollars—some $27 billion annually. We know the still more widespread cost it exacts from millions in fear; fear that can turn us into a nation of captives imprisoned nightly behind chained doors, double locks, barred windows; fear that can make us afraid to walk city streets by night or public parks by day.[15]

The following year, in his special message of February, 1967, he sought to dispel concern that the program he was recommending would ultimately bring about a national police force.

Substantially greater resources must be devoted to improving the entire criminal justice system. The Federal Government must not and will not try to dominate the system. It could not if it tried. Our system of law enforcement is essentially local; based upon local initiative, generated by local energies, and controlled by local officials. But the Federal Government must help to strengthen the system, and to encourage the kind of innovations needed to respond to the problem of crime in America. I recommend that the Congress enact the Safe Streets and Crime Control Act of 1967.[16]

His emphasis was to strengthen *local* efforts and to give *local* agencies direct liaison with the federal government, meaning the Department of Justice.

The commission report only briefly mentioned the possible effects of court decisions on law enforcement. It specifically mentioned the *Gideon* and *Miranda* cases and said that "a man standing alone cannot defend himself adequately against a criminal charge."[17] The recommendation was:

The objective to be met as quickly as possible is to provide

15. Included in the report of the Senate Committee on the Judiciary to accompany S. 917; Report no. 1097, 90th Cong., 2nd sess., p. 30.

16. *Ibid.*, pp. 29, 30.

17. President's Commission, *The Challenge of Crime*, p. 149.

counsel to every criminal defendant who faces a significant penalty, if he cannot afford to provide counsel himself. This should apply to cases classified as misdemeanors
as well as to those classified as felonies. Counsel should be
provided early in the proceedings and certainly no later
than the first judicial appearance. The services of counsel
should be available after conviction through appeal, and
in collateral attack proceedings when issues are not
frivolous. The immediate minimum, until it becomes
possible to provide the foregoing, is that all criminal
defendants who are in danger of substantial loss of liberty
shall be provided with counsel.[18]

The commission also said that it was "too early to assess"
the effect of the *Miranda* decision on the ability of law enforcement personnel to secure confessions in solving crimes. But
this and other decisions "do represent a trend toward findings
by the judiciary that previously permitted police practices are
constitutionally offensive to the dignity and integrity of private
citizens."[19]

But as if to foretell the spirited debate over court decisions
in the Senate the following year, four members of the nineteen-
member commission—with the concurrence of three other
members—presented strong views about the limitations which
had arisen

from the Fifth and Sixth Amendments . . . as they have
been interpreted by the Supreme Court in recent years
. . . there is a serious question, now being increasingly
posed by jurists and scholars, whether some of these
rights have been interpreted and enlarged by Court decision to the point where they now seriously affect the
delicate balance between the rights of the individual and
those of society. Or, putting the question differently,
whether the scales have tilted in favor of the accused and
against law enforcement and the public further than the
best interest of the country permits.[20]

18. *Ibid.*, p. 150.
19. *Ibid.*, p. 94.
20. *Ibid.*, p. 303.

The minority pinpointed the issue in this way:

> . . . in the suddenness of a street encounter, or the con-
> fusion at the scene of a crime, there will be little or no
> opportunity to protect police interrogation against the
> inevitable charge of failing to meet *Miranda* standards.
> The litigation that follows more often than not will be a
> "trial" of the police rather than the accused. . . . Interro-
> gation is the single most essential police procedure. It
> benefits the innocent suspect as much as it aids in ob-
> taining evidence to convict the guilty.[21]

The minority then addressed themselves to the impact of
Miranda on the use of confessions.

> Indeed, this is the other side of the coin. If interrogations
> are muted there will be no confessions; if they are
> tainted, resulting confessions—as well as other related
> evidence—will be excluded or the convictions subse-
> quently set aside. There is real reason for the concern,
> expressed by dissenting justices, that *Miranda* in effect
> proscribes the use of all confessions.[22]

The minority concluded with these words: "Whatever can
be done to right the present imbalance through legislation or
rule of court should have high priority."[23]

These views are significant because the theme was to encourage legislation to "right the present imbalance" and that
is precisely what the Senate Committee on the Judiciary did
in 1968 with its version of the crime bill—some of which
became law. The minority of the commission also had critical
views about the privileges against self-incrimination which

21. *Ibid.*, p. 305.
22. *Ibid.*
23. *Ibid.*, p. 307. The four authors of the minority presentation
were all attorneys. All had former military service and experience in
law enforcement. One of the concurring members was the attorney
general of California; one was a chief of police; and the third had just
completed a term as president of the National District Attorneys
Association.

were applicable to the states. "Plainly this is an area requiring the most thoughtful attention."[24] The group expressed some doubts, however, that legislation or a rule of court would right the imbalance. "If, as now appears likely, a constitutional amendment is required to strengthen law enforcement in these respects, the American people should face up to the need and undertake necessary action without delay."[25]

THE HEARINGS: HOUSE

The president's proposals were reflected in H.R. 5037 introduced on February 8, 1967, by Representative Emanuel Celler (Dem.) of New York, the chairman of the Committee on the Judiciary. An identical bill was S. 917 introduced in the Senate the same day by Senator John L. McClellan (Dem.) of Arkansas, the chairman of the Sul,committee on Criminal Laws and Procedures of the Senate Committee on the Judiciary.[26]
House subcommittee hearings began in March, and were under the chairmanship of Representative Celler. He set the tone for the hearings saying of the administration bill that "it

24. *Ibid.*, p. 306.
25. *Ibid.*, p. 308. Senator Sam J. Ervin, Jr. (Dem.) of North Carolina was to oblige them with his Senate Joint Resolution 22, proposing a constitutional amendment that confessions be admissible in evidence in all criminal prosecutions if found by the trial court to have been given voluntarily, and restricting the jurisdiction of the Supreme Court and other federal courts to reverse or otherwise disturb a ruling by a trial court admitting a confession in evidence as voluntary if the ruling is supported by competent evidence. He later changed his mind and was able to get the substance of his proposal in the Senate Committee version of the omnibus crime control and safe streets bill.
26. Sponsorship also included Senators Ervin, Philip A. Hart (Dem.) of Michigan, Roman Hruska (Rep.) of Nebraska, Hugh Scott (Rep.) of Pennsylvania, Robert C. Byrd (Dem.) of West Virginia, Jacob K. Javits (Rep.) of New York, and Fred R. Harris (Dem.) of Oklahoma.

established within the Department of Justice a Director of a New Office of Law Enforcement and Criminal Justice Assistance. This agency will provide a very necessary means to bring about the cooperation of State and local law enforcement agencies to promote criminal justice as well as prevent crime.'' [27]

The subcommittee had thirty-one bills related to crime control although several were duplicative. Most of them dealt with subjects raised by the commission or from the president's recommendations. Most of the hearings centered on the titles of the administration bill and those on eavesdropping and wire tapping. One member of the subcommittee, Representative Robert McClory (Rep.) of Illinois, wanted to broaden the scope of the hearings by having his bills and related measures included. These were directed for the most part to the issues surrounding *Mallory* and *Miranda*. On the first day of the hearings, he said:

> It seems to me unfortunate, though, that we do not have some legislation recommended by the Administration which would help to overcome some recent U.S. Supreme Court decisions. . . . I would hope that in the course of these hearings the Attorney General would cooperate with this committee to seek such legislative or constitutional changes as may be necessary in order to facilitate criminal prosecutions, particularly with respect to securing the benefit of voluntary confessions. . . .[28]

To this Representative Celler replied:

> I will say to the gentlemen that there is a slight difference of opinion whether we should consider that particular bill, which Mr. McClory introduced in these hearings. It is the purpose of the Chair to take up those bills at a subsequent period after we have concluded the hearings on the general crime.[29]

27. House subcommittee, *1967 Hearings*, p. 22. There was also a provision on firearms control.

28. *Ibid.*, p. 27.

29. *Ibid.*, p. 28. These bills were considered during the last two days of the 1967 hearings.

Celler conducted the hearings as he said he would, but there were frequent questions of some witnesses about the Court decisions. The first witness was Attorney General Ramsey Clark. In the course of the questioning, Representative James C. Corman (Dem.) of California asked him if there was any statistical evidence of an increase in crime as a result of the "court's decision circumscribing the uses of confessions." Clark's response was as follows:

> No. . . . I think there is a whole lot of statistical data that is subject to many different interpretations on that. I think unfortunately we have so enlarged and so dramatized the role of confessions in the total criminal justice process that we have lost our sense of proportion about it.
> REPRESENTATIVE CORMAN: I think we are building a strawman when we try to build up the court as the cause of crime and the difficulty of law enforcement.[30]

Later Representative Peter W. Rodino (Dem.) of New Jersey asked Clark if he thought changes in the Constitution would be necessary to have effective control over crime and violence. Clark responded:

> No, I do not. I just do not think that anything approaching a case for that has been made at this time. Here is a very impressive fact to me. I think it speaks volumes about this problem. They are talking about the *Miranda* decision. Since 1948 the Federal Bureau of Investigation has given a warning, or whatever you want to call it, to people that it is going to interrogate that is very, very similar to what is required under *Miranda*. It has been essentially the same since 1948. The FBI has not said we can't live with this. We can't enforce the laws with this. We can't protect the public with this. Their conviction rate in their cases prosecuted in courts in the first 6 months of this fiscal year is 97 percent. The guilty plea rate in those same cases is 87 or 88 percent. I do not think I am boasting because I have not contributed to the FBI, but I think this shows what excellence in training, in developing personnel, in setting standards for personnel, can do to law enforcement. I think this is the answer.[31]

30. *Ibid.*, p. 45.
31. *Ibid.*, p. 49.

The administration proposal was directed to upgrading local personnel involved in law enforcement, not to changing Court decisions.

Notwithstanding chairman Celler's admonition earlier to Representative McClory, the subject of the effects of Court decisions on crime was raised. McClory took the occasion after Clark's comment to express his disagreement and raised the question of the minority report of the commission about *Miranda*.

> Mr. Chairman, I do not want to get into a full dress discussion of *Miranda*, except to bring out, if I may, that law enforcement officials and respected individuals have called my attention, and I am sure called to the attention of the public, that the effect of those decisions is to seriously hamper the investigation and prosecution of crime. I think the committee should take that into consideration.[32]

To which the chairman replied: "That is a conclusion with which we disagree."[33]

But on March 23, when Superintendent O. W. Wilson of the Chicago Police Department was a witness, Representative McClory inquired of him what the function or responsibility the subcommittee should assume about legislation intended to modify *Miranda* and related cases. His response was: "I don't understand how Congress or State legislators can change this decision short of constitutional amendment."[34] But he gave support to Representative McClory's views. "It appears that the *Miranda* decision has almost, if not completely, taken the police out of the inquiry system."[35] Chairman Celler then sought to end that aspect of the inquiry.

> If we are going to allow the police all over the country to extract confessions without the presence of counsel, and there is long delay between the time of the arrest and the time of arraignment, I think we are getting back to that

32. *Ibid.*, pp. 71, 72.
33. *Ibid.*, p. 72.
34. *Ibid.*, p. 404.
35. *Ibid.*

which is very much akin, though not exactly so, to the thumbscrew and the rack and the truncheon; only in a different form, that is all. And that is why we have the fifth amendment and the decisions of the Court.[36]

On April 26, 1967, next to the last day of the hearings, Representative Richard H. Poff (Rep.) of Virginia appeared and discussed commission proposals and suggested other items which neither the president nor the commission adopted. These were to counter the *Miranda, Escobedo, McNabb,* and *Mallory* decisions.[37]

Another witness toward the end of the hearings, was Representative Robert A. Taft, Jr., (Rep.) of Ohio. He directed his attention to proposed legislation which would regulate criminal interrogation. "I propose that we establish clearer standards than the flat fiat of Miranda." And of *Mallory,* he said, "I have stayed within" the *Mallory* rule.[38]

The testimony and comments of one of the last witnesses is pertinent. William J. Campbell, chief judge, U.S. District for the Northern District of Illinois, urged the adoption of legislation which would restore "to the law of custodial confessions a system similar to that which I felt was in the main successful, practical, and fairly administered in our courts for many years, a system either eliminated or at least seriously questioned by the Supreme Court in *Miranda.*"[39]

THE HEARINGS: SENATE

The Senate subcommittee hearings were under the direction of the chairman, Senator McClellan. They began on March 7, 1967, and were concluded July 12 the same year. Sixteen bills were officially before the subcommittee.

36. *Ibid.*, p. 405.
37. *Ibid.*, p. 1418.
38. *Ibid.*, p. 1462. One of the last witnesses was Representative Jack Edwards (Rep.) of Alabama, who introduced a bill (H.R. 6709) identical to Senator McClellan's S. 674 on admissibility of confessions. Other bills before the subcommittee which had only brief presentations also related to confessions.
39. *Ibid.*, p. 1497.

The Senate hearings were in marked contrast to those of the House. Whereas Representative Celler directed the efforts of his subcommittee to the administration's proposals, Senator McClellan said the first day that three bills would be of especial importance. One was his S. 674 concerning the admissibility in evidence of confessions; one was on wire-tapping, and one intended to "outlaw the Mafia and other organized crime syndicates."[40] He listed S. 917, the administration's Safe Streets and Crime Control Act as "another of the bills to be considered." It was clear at the outset that McClellan considered the administration bill of far less importance than the first three he mentioned. It was clear also that the hearings would center on proposals to "overrule" decisions of the U.S. Supreme Court. Senator Sam J. Ervin, Jr. (Dem.) of North Carolina and member of the subcommittee put it this way: "I have, therefore, expressed the opinion that it will require either some judicial repentance, which I consider unlikely, or a constitutional amendment to protect the American people from the consequences of those rulings."[41] He also said that he thought another route was available, to restrict the appellate jurisdiction of the Supreme Court and the inferior federal appellate courts.

McClellan indicated there were four remedies open to the subcommittee: enact his S. 674 relating to confessions, a constitutional amendment which was suggested by Senator Ervin and the substance of S. 674, restrict the appellate jurisdiction of the federal courts to prevent them from considering whether a confession was voluntary, or doing nothing.

This, then, was the climate for the 1967 Senate hearings which took ten days.

As was brought out the following year during the debate on the Senate floor, virtually all of the witnesses who appeared before the subcommittee were hostile to the Supreme Court decisions and strong supporters of one or more of the bills

40. *Hearings before the Subcommittee on Criminal Laws and Procedures of the Senate Committee on the Judiciary*, 90th Cong. 1st sess. (1967), p. 2.
41. *Ibid.*, pp. 4, 5.

given priority by McClellan. Several witnesses supported the administration proposal and except for changing the system for grants, that proposal encountered no serious difficulty during House consideration later that year.

An early witness was Senator John Stennis (Dem.) of Mississippi. The substance of his presentation was "the dangerous trend" which he believed would "continue at an accelerated pace under this 5–4 *Miranda* decision, unless something is done about it."[42]

Throughout the hearings and during the Senate debate reference was made to the 5–4 decision in *Miranda*, the vote of one justice which was the root of the problem. Proponents of the measures intended to overrule the Supreme Court in one way or another found comfort in the dissenting opinions of the four justices. Some support to the McClellan-Ervin position was given by Senator Alan Bible (Dem.) of Nevada, who recited his work as the chairman of the Senate Committee for the District of Columbia. That committee had addressed itself to the problem of crime in the district and had included in a bill in 1966, vetoed by the president, a six-hour outside limit on detaining a suspect for questioning before arraignment. Bible said: "It was the view of the members of my Committee, in their careful consideration of procedures to modify *Mallory*, some time period be included, so that police officers would be unable to detain a defendant in police custody for an indefinite period of time."[43]

When asked if he believed the *Mallory* rule was a contributing factor in the increase in crime rates in the district, Bible said:

> Personally I think *Mallory* had an adverse effect on law enforcement. . . . It seems to me we have become obsessed with uncovering new rights and safeguards for the criminal to such a degree that we have unbalanced the scales of justice, and find ourselves in the unenviable position of losing control of the crime and violence that are running

42. *Ibid.*, p. 114.
43. *Ibid.*, p. 133

rampant in our cities. . . . I think there are those in the field of criminology who would testify that this in itself wasn't the main factor, that there were psychological factors, there was the upbringing of the fatherless child in the District of Columbia who had no place to go and no playground to play on and no recreation and no job opportunities. I recognize these as long-range factors.[44]

These latter references to some fundamental causes of crime—well expressed in the crime commission report, were rarely mentioned in the hearings or during Senate debate.

Some witnesses were quite emotional in discussing the conditions they believed could be corrected only by strong measures. One was Senator Frank J. Lausche (Dem.) of Ohio, who said that "if we want to aggravate the fear and trepidation of the women in our homes, keep the *Miranda* law in effect; on the other hand, if law and order is to be maintained the Congress should take action to nullify that decision."[45]

Similar statements permeated the course of the hearings. They evidenced a deep concern and frustration about crime, a growing fear among much of the population about urban unrest, but they also emphasized a desire to control it by the expedient of returning to "a proper balance" between the rights of an accused and the interests of society, and to restore practices in effect prior to *Mallory* and *Miranda*. This was the proper route for "law and order."

The witnesses whose views are included in this chapter frequently repeated what other witnesses stated, but in order to present the direction of the hearings, the main force and purpose, and the central theme of a variety of individuals, a number of those views are pertinent. They reinforced the views of the majority of the members of the subcommittee and also reflected the judgments of many who had experience in law enforcement. Unfortunately, as indicated elsewhere, there was no apparent effort by Senator McClellan to obtain the

44. *Ibid.*, pp. 131, 132.
45. *Ibid.*, p. 141.

views of those who supported the substance of the Court decisions he sought to eliminate. The hearings were hardly balanced in that respect.

One witness placed a measure of blame on the Congress and the state legislatures for the predicament they now faced. Judge J. Edward Lumbard, chief judge of the U.S. Court of Appeals, Second District of New York, made these comments: "If the Congress finds that the application of the Supreme Court decision in the *Miranda* cases is seriously interfering with the obtaining of voluntary statements by Federal and State law enforcement officers, the only way to correct the situation would be by amendment of the Constitution." But he appeared to feel that the decisions under attack came about because of prior legislative indifference.

> As I said before, it is because the Congress and the legislatures of the States have taken so little action in the field of criminal justice that the courts have more and more chosen to lay down rules which have the force of law until changed, and which all too frequently come to us in the form of new constitutional principles which then can be modified only by constitutional amendment.[46]

Throughout the hearings and later during the Senate debate, Senator McClellan insisted that he did not want to "correct" the Court decisions by constitutional amendment.

> It is certainly at best a cumbersome process, very nearly impossible of achievement as far as the machinery of government is concerned. In addition to being cumbersome, it takes quite some time to put a constitutional amendment through. In the meantime, pending that, you have the present law, as enunciated by the Supreme Court, which would prevail.[47]

It was McClellan's contention that the evils of the decisions had to be dealt with immediately. A delay would be intolerable. Anyway, he voiced hope that the members of the

46. *Ibid.*, p. 184.
47. *Ibid.*, p. 185.

majority of the Supreme Court "might change their position" or at least one might change "on the side of law and order instead of continuing to insist on a position that obviously does work to the advantage of criminals." [48]

In an exchange between Senator Ervin and Judge Lumbard, the senator sought support for his position that prior to *Escobedo*—which made a "quicksand" of the Sixth Amendment—a suspect would have to have counsel only when prosecution was begun. But the judge observed that the circumstances were that Escobedo was then in custody of the police, had asked for his lawyer who was in the stationhouse, but was denied it. Ervin then turned to the use of confessions which were voluntarily given.

> So under the law as it existed before the *Miranda* case no man could be convicted of any crime merely upon his own confession that he committed the crime. In other words, before he could be convicted, it would have to be shown by evidence outside of his voluntary confession, beyond a reasonable doubt, that a crime had been committed.
>
> JUDGE LUMBARD: I can't remember any case in recent times, Senator, where a man has been convicted in this country solely on his own confession. [49]

Senator Ervin indicated that his bill to restrict the appellate jurisdiction of the federal courts to inquire into the voluntariness of a confession admitted in evidence, if sustained by the highest appellate state court having jurisdiction, would place responsibility where it belonged and not in some review court far removed from the first hand knowledge of the trial judge and jury. This became a part of the committee bill, reported to the Senate the following year.

Many objections to the standards announced in *Miranda* were that they were too strict and had the effect of having no interrogation at all. Senator Ervin put it this way: "I have to confess from my experience I believe neither the Congress nor the Supreme Court nor anybody else could ever be smart

48. *Ibid.*, p. 180.
49. *Ibid.*, p. 189.

enough to devise any rules more calculated to prevent anybody from ever confessing their guilt than those laid down in
the *Miranda* decision." [50]

Presumably the senator was saying that notwithstanding the
invitation by the Supreme Court to devise alternatives to the
four standards in *Miranda*, anything less stringent would be
unacceptable to the Court. Therefore, the dilemma was to be
resolved by preventing a review of the observance of those
standards by the federal courts, including the Supreme Court.

Major support of the McClellan-Ervin position came from
prosecutors. One was Arlen Spector, district attorney for the
city and county of Philadelphia. He presented statistics which
indicated 59 percent of those arrested refused to give a statement after the *Miranda* warnings, whereas prior to it only 32
percent failed to give statements. This kind of testimony
obviously strengthened the arguments against *Miranda*. [51] These
data did not indicate the extent to which they were comparable in types of crimes, characteristics and background of
those accused, or whether other factors than *Miranda* warnings
affected the percentages. Spector did not, however, want to
cast *Miranda* standards aside. Nor did he believe a constitutional amendment should be adopted which would limit the
authority of the Supreme Court to rule on questions of procedure under the Due Process Clause of the Fourteenth
Amendment. "It would be highly dangerous to alter generally
the authority of the Supreme Court to review state criminal
proceedings." [52]

Spector supported only three of the standards, however.
These were the right to remain silent; that anything said
could be used against an accused; and the right to have the
advice of a lawyer. To him, the problem was the fourth
standard. It was the "fictional stone" and one he claimed
would "sink" and that the Supreme Court would have to
step aside one way or another. The question of the voluntariness of a statement, he said, should be determined by the

50. *Ibid.*, p. 196.
51. *Ibid.*, pp. 200, 201.
52. *Ibid.*, p. 202.

trial court. He said he also believed the Congress had the power to exclude the last warning from the protections against self-incrimination by reason of section five of the Fourteenth Amendment. This reads: "The Congress shall have power to enforce, by appropriate legislation, the provisions of this article." This also was the view of Senator Ervin.[53]

McClellan's S. 674 affected federal prosecutions only, but the district attorney of Kings County, New York, Arron E. Koota, believed that it would have an immediate impact on state procedures.

> Underlying the *Miranda* rule is the fifth amendment privilege against self-incrimination, which is now binding upon the States. In *Malloy* v. *Hogan*, the Supreme Court declared the Federal standards for the determination of the scope and interpretation of this privilege shall be adhered to by the States. Senate bill 674 established criteria of confessional admissibility which would perforce be followed by State legislatures or their judiciary.[54]

Thus, if the transgressions imposed were taken from the federal procedures, there would be no barrier to state action.

Some witnesses referred to the intent of the founding fathers. One was James T. Wilkinson, commonwealth attorney for Richmond, Virginia.

> SENATOR ERVIN: The Constitution is supposed to be, was intended to be, the most stable of all legal documents in this country, wasn't it?
> MR. WILKINSON: Yes, sir.
> SENATOR ERVIN: And starting with the *Mapp* case in 1961 down to date through *Escobedo* and the *Miranda* case, it is as constant as a quivering aspen leaf.[55]

Two members of the subcommittee who differed with the majority on the proposed legislation were Senators Edward M. Kennedy (Dem.) of Massachusetts, and Philip A. Hart (Dem.) of Michigan. Senator Kennedy sought to obtain a delay in the

53. *Ibid.*, pp. 203, 204.
54. *Ibid.*, p. 233.
55. *Ibid.*, p. 257. *Mapp* v. *Ohio*. 367 U.S. 643.

legislation proposed to counter *Mallory* and *Miranda* and related decisions until there was more evidence of the adverse effect they had in fact. "We just haven't got the statistics and the facts to make what many of us consider to be an extraordinary step with regard to an individual's need to be aware of his rights, and his need to be represented by competent counsel in court."[56]

Senator Hart, in querying one witness, said:

> Is it fair for me to summarize my understanding of your testimony with respect to *Miranda*, that at this time you are not in a position to tell us one case you have lost because of *Miranda*, and second, that you feel it is too early to make any judgment with respect to the course of action which you take?
>
> MR. GIRARDIN: Yes, that is a fair summary.[57]

This was part of the police commissioner's statement that "a hardened criminal never told us anything anyway unless he was in such a position that he tried to make a deal. By a 'deal' I mean if he would tell us something we didn't know, usually on someone else, we would go a little easier on him."[58]

Senator McClellan's concern about rising crime rates and his unswerving stand that the Supreme Court decisions had a disastrous impact upon effective police methods caused him to react to Girardin's statement in this way.

> You talk about this *Miranda* decision having no impact. Let me ask you this. Do you doubt that the *Miranda* decision is causing cases to be dismissed where the defendant is absolutely guilty?

56. *Ibid.*, pp. 287, 288.

57. *Ibid.*, pp. 314, 315. The witness was Ray Girardin, police commissioner, Detroit, Michigan. One of the few other witnesses who urged the subcommittee to get more facts was Senator Joseph D. Tydings (Dem.) of Maryland. He was a member of the full committee, but not the subcommittee. He later served as the floor leader to oppose Title II. He urged the subcommittee to get facts rather than "just statements and judgments which are not based on facts." *Ibid.*, p. 862.

58. *Ibid.*, p. 314.

MR. GIRARDIN: Senator, as I said, I don't know of a single case. It may, it may not. I would like more time to gather statistics and see what effect it has. ... That I don't know a specific outstanding case in my district where we could attribute it to the *Miranda* case.[59]

The testimony of most witnesses countered such suggestions about not enough data to warrant the proposals being considered by the subcommittee. For example, the executive director of the International Association of Chiefs of Police added support to the plans to "curb" the Court with the following:

> We are confused because it seems that as greatly as the executive and legislative branches toil to help the police and to bring about a decrease in crime, the judicial branch (in the form of our U.S. Supreme Court) appears to be applying itself just as assiduously to stripping the police of their traditional, time-tested, and previously acceptable devices and techniques for combating crime. ... I do want to mention one aspect, however, which may not have been considered, and this is the effect of such Supreme Court decisions on police attitudes and morale. I submit that no man will continue to try to do the best job he can when, day by day, the means of performing that job are being withdrawn. ... Coping with it is becoming even more complicated, and the police are now surrounded by such a murky atmosphere of court decision and judicial indecision that about the only type of crime they can take decisive action on is the crime of violence which occurs before their very eyes.[60]

Exaggerated or not, this was the belief of an able witness. But the extent to which that and much of the other testimony was needed to bolster the previously conceived position taken by Senator McClellan and Senator Ervin especially, is not known, but it indicates that even if the *Mallory* and *Miranda* decisions did make it more difficult to control crime because the traditional and time-tested methods were challenged, the

59. *Ibid.*, pp. 317, 318.
60. *Ibid.*, pp. 328, 329.

International Association of Chiefs of Police were not supporting steps to try to comply with the newer rules. The choice appeared to be to cry that the police were helpless. True, the gathering of evidence can be complicated and difficult and requires at least as much talent on the part of the police as on the one who committed the crime and left the evidence. This was fundamental to the president's proposals on police training and the provisions for support to upgrade police standards.

The trial judge at the second *Miranda* trial testified before the subcommittee on April 19, 1967.

> JUDGE WREN: I was called to Phoenix from the northern part of the State to sit on the retrial of *Miranda*. I would like to add, gentlemen, that it was quite an experience. The retrial itself portrays my concern with its doctrine, and the problems which the Supreme Court decision places before us.
> A jury was finally impaneled and immediately thereafter sequestered at the demand of defense counsel, Mr. John Flynn. He thereupon filed a motion to suppress certain evidence, as he is entitled to do under both Arizona and Federal law. And what followed, gentlemen, was a 9-day game of constitutional chess, during which time the jurors, during the 9 days, heard only 6 hours of testimony. The rules of this game were so complex and the publicity on the excluded confession so intense that the jury was locked up in a motel room where they had no access whatsoever to the news media. . . . Miranda would have gone free on his second trial, because of the exclusionary ruling, on an instructed verdict of acquittal had not the county attorney's office, 1 week before the second trial, literally stumbled onto a statement made by the accused to a woman with whom he had been living at the time of the rape.[61]

So deeply felt was the judge's opposition to the *Miranda* decision that he made this statement to the subcommittee. "Miranda was convicted at the second trial, and, in a way,

61. *Ibid.*, p. 527.

this was unfortunate, because it lends credence to the Supreme Court's statement that without the confession to police there was still adequate evidence."[62]

On March 18, 1967, the National District Attorney's Association, meeting in Los Angeles, adopted the following resolution:

> Where the *Miranda* v. *Arizona* case introduced new principles of law dealing with the use of confessions and admissions in the prosecution of criminal cases,
> Whereas for many years the law of our nation had applied a test of voluntariness to the admissibility of admissions and confessions, and
> Whereas these new principles enunciated in *Miranda* v. *Arizona* are very restrictive and have had serious impact on the prosecution of criminal cases and on law enforcement throughout the nation, and Whereas, Legislation is needed to restore the voluntary test in the federal and state courts, and
> Whereas, such legislation is in the best interest of the law-abiding citizens and reflects the national consensus on what constitutes fundamental fairness as envisioned by the due process clause of the Fourteenth Amendment and would, therefore, beneficially affect state actions.
> *Therefore be it resolved* that the . . . Association . . . unanimously urges appropriate legislation to accomplish the purpose herein stated.[63]

The proposals urged by Senators McClellan and Ervin could be considered as threats, and this was illustrated again and again by Senator McClellan. Toward the end of the hearings, he said: "I had hoped, and I still hope, that we can work out in this committee a bill that will be held constitutional by the Supreme Court. Some member of the Court may have to change his mind a bit, and upon reflection there is plenty of room for a change of mind, in my opinion."[64]

The last witness to appear before the subcommittee was Lawrence Speiser, director, Washington office, of the American

62. *Ibid.*, p. 529.
63. *Ibid.*, pp. 619, 620.
64. *Ibid.*, p. 849.

Civil Liberties Union. He was one of the few who appeared before the committee opposed to the McClellan-Ervin proposals.

> All of these attempts to overturn *Miranda* by legislation, and I do not believe that can be done. They attempt to undercut the *Mallory* rule. . . . Although the Supreme Court has not specifically ruled on the constitutional standing of *Mallory*, simply because they had had rule 5(a) on which to base it, they would hold that the *Mallory* rule does have a constitutional basis as a means of preventing denial of·counsel, as a means of insuring that individuals have a proper protection against illegal arrests and, of course, confessions. . . . Third, we oppose attempts to restrict appellate review by the U.S. Supreme Court as a threat to the independence of the judiciary.[65]

Speiser also said that "we do not feel that the confession problem has any effect or much effect, if any, on the question of crime in the United States."[66] McClellan's response was the one he usually gave to any who disagreed with him: his proposals were the only remedies, short of a constitutional amendment—unless one judge would change his mind. He insisted that his disagreement with the Supreme Court was not a personal matter, "but if the Supreme Court is wrong in what it is doing or assuming under the Constitution as written at present, if the procedure that it is requiring now is an obstruction to law enforcement and if it hampers the apprehension and protection [*sic*] of criminals, I think it should be remedied if we can remedy it, because I think it does incalculable harm to our country."[67] A further clue to his strategy were these words: "The Supreme Court changes. You cannot depend on it being stable. I hope we get men on the Court in time who will decide that this Court was wrong. I hope it will become a reality and not only a probability."[68]

65. *Ibid.*, p. 1173.
66. *Ibid.*, p. 1174.
67. *Ibid.*, pp. 1174, 1175.
68. *Ibid.*, p. 1175.

Whether hearings on proposed legislation weigh heavily on the outcome can be seriously questioned. On the crime bill, the House subcommittee hearings were primarily explanatory discourses supporting the essentials of the administration proposals, although there were opposition witnesses to several details. The subcommittee's endorsement of the bill, even with several amendments, did not alter the original bill in substance. It contained nothing about confessions, the right to counsel, time delays prior to arraignment, or the restrictions on the appellate jurisdiction of the federal courts as did the Senate version. Representative Celler, chairman of the subcommittee, was also chairman of the full committee, and he apparently had little difficulty in obtaining a majority favorable to the administration proposals. There were, as can be expected, minority views. Twelve of the fifteen Republican members signed minority views, with several individual positions being recorded.[69]

The committee system of the Congress—or of a state legislature—is frequently referred to as providing "little legislatures." It is also often criticized as unduly fragmenting the legislative process and as one which encourages logrolling with many dozens of subcommittees, each of which may have a chairman who is not the full committee chairman. It is also said that this fragmentation discourages or even prevents members of a legislative body from having much familiarity with the total legislative product.

But no acceptable or workable substitute has been devised. The number of full committees in the House and Senate were reduced after World War II, but the number of subcommittees has not lessened. Unquestionably, with all its faults, the subcommittee system is essential if the vast and complex volume of proposals is to be handled. Time alone would make it virtually impossible for an individual member to give attention to more than a mere handful of proposals were it not for the committee-subcommittee system. On the favorable side

69. Report no. 488 to accompany H.R. 5037, 90th Cong., 1st sess. (July 17, 1967).

the system does produce many experts who are obviously essential to producing a satisfactory legislative product.

Since members of the Congress have several subcommittee assignments and other obligations which compete for their time, absenteeism may be high. Similarly, it is a common practice for a subcommittee report to be made orally to a full (parent) committee and the full membership of either the subcommittee or the full committee may not have the printed details of the hearings or reports until long afterward. Another characteristic of the subcommittee system is that the subcommittee chairman would not last long in that position if he did not have the confidence of the chairman of the parent committee and in all likelihood the two agree upon the oral report well in advance of its presentation.

These circumstances can be related to the crime bill. The House subcommittee hearings were concluded on April 27, 1967. The printed report to accompany H.R. 5037 is dated July 17, 1967.[70] The time factor was different in the Senate. The hearings were concluded on July 12, 1967, but the printed report to accompany S. 917 is dated April 29, 1968.[71]

The subcommittee of the House had thirteen members, with thirty-five forming the full committee. Since H.R. 5037 did not contain the features of Title II of the Senate version of the crime bill, no further consideration of the House subcommittee or committee action is essential here.

The Senate subcommittee was composed of five Democrats and three Republicans.[72] Senator McClellan presided over all ten meetings. No other member of the subcommittee is recorded present for all sessions. Senator James C. Eastland (Dem.) of Mississippi, chairman of the full committee, is not recorded as attending any of the public hearings, although he participated in the executive sessions later in the year. Senator

70. The report, together with "Supplemental and Additional Views" is forty-six pages in length.

71. The Senate committee report is 284 pages in length.

72. The Democrats were Senators McClellan, Ervin, Hart, Eastland, and Kennedy; the Republicans, Senators Hruska, Scott, and Thurmond.

Ervin attended six meetings; Senator Hart, five; Senator Roman Hruska (Rep.) of Nebraska, six; Senator Hugh Scott (Rep.) of Pennsylvania, three; Senator Strom Thurmond (Rep.) of South Carolina, four; and Senator Kennedy, seven. Most of the participation was limited to Senators McClellan and Ervin as related to Title II. The report to accompany S. 917, however, includes objections to Title II by Senators Hart and Kennedy of the subcommittee, joined by Senators Joseph D. Tydings, Thomas J. Dodd (Dem.) of Connecticut, Edward V. Long (Dem.) of Missouri, Quentin N. Burdick (Dem.) of North Dakota, Hiram L. Fong (Rep.) of Hawaii, and Birch Bayh (Dem.) of Indiana. The committee bill was obviously the product of the persistent efforts of Senator McClellan and Senator Ervin, with more than adequate support from the other southern senators and most of the Republicans on the committee.

During September and October, 1967, Senator McClellan held several executive sessions of the subcommittee designed to consolidate the proposals he and Senator Ervin supported and to report them to the full committee. Senators Hart and Kennedy tried to delay action believing that time and more reflection would make their views prevail. They failed, even though narrowly, and with the last minute support of Senator Scott, the McClellan-Ervin version was adopted and became Title II of S. 917. That title read as follows:

Title II—Admissibility of Confessions, Reviewability of Admission in Evidence of Confessions in State Cases, Admissibility in Evidence of Eye Witness Testimony, and Procedures in Obtaining Writs of Habeas Corpus

3501. Admissibility of confessions

(a) In any criminal prosecution brought by the United States or by the District of Columbia, a confession, as defined in subsection (e) hereof, shall be admissible in evidence if it is voluntarily given. Before such confession is received in evidence, the trial judge shall, out of the presence of the jury, determine any issue as to voluntariness. If the trial judge determines that the confession was voluntarily made it shall be admitted in evidence and the trial judge shall permit the jury to hear relevant evidence on the issue of voluntariness and shall instruct the jury to give such weight to the confession as the jury feels it deserves under all the circumstances.

(b) The trial judge in determining the issue of voluntariness shall take into consideration all the circumstances surrounding the giving of the confession, including (1) the time elapsing between arrest and arraignment of the defendant making the confession, if it was made after arrest and before arraignment, (2) whether such defendant knew the nature of the offense with which he was charged or of which he was suspected at the time of making the confession, (3) whether or not such defendant was advised or knew that he was not required to make any statement and that any such statement could be used against him, (4) whether or not such defendant had been advised prior to questioning of his right to the assistance of counsel; and (5) whether or not such defendant was without the assistance of counsel when questioned and when giving such confession. The presence or absence of any of the above-mentioned factors to be taken into consideration by the judge need not be conclusive on the issue of voluntariness of the confession.

(c) In any criminal prosecution by the United States or by the District of Columbia, a confession made or given by a person who is a defendant therein, while such person was under arrest or other detention in the custody of any law-enforcement officer or law-enforcement agency, shall not be inadmissible solely because of delay in bringing such person before a commissioner or other officer empowered to commit persons charged with offenses against the laws of the United States or of the District of Columbia if such confession is found by the trial judge to have been made voluntarily and if the weight to be given the confession is left to the jury.

(d) Nothing contained in this section shall bar the admission in evidence of any confession made or given voluntarily by any person to any other person without interrogation by anyone, or at any time at which the person who made or gave such confession was not under arrest or other detention.

(e) As used in this section, the term "confession"

means any confession of guilt of any criminal offense or
any self-incriminating statement made or given orally or
in writing.

3502. Reviewability of admission in evidence of confessions in State cases

Neither the Supreme Court nor any inferior court
ordained and established by Congress under article III
of the Constitution of the United States shall have jurisdiction to review or to reverse, vacate, modify, or disturb
in any way, a ruling of any trial court of any State in any
criminal prosecution admitting in evidence as voluntarily made an admission or confession of an accused if
such ruling has been affirmed or otherwise upheld by the
highest court of the State having appellate jurisdiction of
the cause.

3503. Admissibility in evidence of eye witness testimony

The testimony of a witness that he saw the accused
commit or participate in the commission of the crime for
which the accused is being tried shall be admissible into
evidence in a criminal prosecution in any trial court
ordained and established under article III of the Constitution of the United States; and neither the Supreme
Court nor any inferior appellate court ordained and
established by the Congress under article III of the Constitution of the United States shall have jurisdiction to
review, reverse, vacate, modify, or disturb in any way a
ruling of such a trial court or any trial court in any State,
territory, district, commonwealth, or other possession of
the United States admitting in evidence in any criminal
prosecution the testimony of a witness that he saw the
accused commit or participate in the commission of the
crime for which the accused is tried.

2256. Procedures in obtaining writs of habeas corpus

The judgment of a court of a State upon a plea or verdict
of guilty in a criminal action, shall be conclusive with
respect to all questions of law or fact which were determined, or which could have been determined, in that
action until such judgment is reversed, vacated, or modified by a court having jurisdiction to review by appeal or
certiorari such judgment; and neither the Supreme Court
nor any inferior court ordained and established by

Congress under article III of the Constitution of the United States shall have jurisdiction to reverse, vacate, nor modify any such judgment of a State court except upon appeal from, or writ of certiorari granted to review, a determination made with respect to such judgment upon review thereof by the highest court of that State having jurisdiction to review such judgment.

This was the Senate Committee version of S. 917 (Title II), but both it and the report were not available to the full Senate (or the public) until debate was ready to begin on May 1, 1968.[73]

73. Senate approval to print was obtained on April 29, 1968.

V

Debate and Passage

The House of Representatives commenced debate on H.R. 5037 on August 2, 1967. It was passed after floor amendments on August 8, 1967.

Although the original bill was given some rewriting by the subcommittee and more on the floor, the major change was in the allocation of funds to local communities. The House insisted on block grants to the states which in turn would allocate funds to the local governmental agencies. Supporters of the direct grant plan—the president's proposal—claimed that allocations first to the states would delay use of the funds and even if not the funds might not go to the communities needing the money most or to those having the "innovative" programs. Those urging the block grant approach to the states were critical of the Department of Justice which would manage the funds appropriated. There were claims that this would concentrate undue power in the attorney general and might result in the establishment of a national police force. Others objected during House debate that the direct grant plan would give the attorney general power to withhold grants because of guidelines unacceptable to local communities.[1]

Representative L. Mendel Rivers (Dem.) of South Carolina said during House debate that "I am losing confidence in the Department of Justice . . . I am charging the decisionmaking officials at Justice with ignoring their responsibility to society

1. *Congressional Record*, 90th Cong., 1st sess., August 2, 1967, 21095.

and to the American people in order not to offend certain minority groups." [2]

On a roll call vote, a heavy majority approved block grants. The vote was 256 to 147.[3] On the final vote for passage only 23 House members opposed the bill. The House thereby ignored the strong opposition to block grants by the International Conference of Police Associations, the National League of Cities, and a host of local government officials who evidenced little enthusiasm over the prospects of state control over funds.[4]

Throughout the debate while the House was sitting as the committee of the Whole House and later in the House, per se, little was said about the legislation proposed by Senators McClellan and Ervin seeking to curb the Supreme Court. One comment, however, came from Representative Watkins M. Abbitt (Dem.) of Virginia, who said: "Apparently the majority of the members of the Supreme Court of America [sic] are more interested in protecting the lawless than they are in preserving law and order. . . . We have no hope of stopping crime until the peace officers are given the necessary right to enforce the laws. . . ." [5]

Another criticism came from Representative F. Edward Hebert (Dem.) of Louisiana: "The gentleman has referred to the poor results—as related to the police. It is a wonder they can arrest anyone—that the police can arrest anyone—under the rulings of the present Supreme Court." [6]

During the debate it was urged that the crime bill would not end crime since much crime was caused by such social ills as poor living conditions. This prompted Representative Paul A. Fino (Rep.) of New York to exclaim:

Frankly, I am sick and tired of having the recent riots blamed on poor housing. . . . No matter where I go in my

2. *Congressional Record*, 90th Cong., 1st sess., August 8, 1967, 21832.
3. *Ibid.*, 21859, 21860.
4. *Congressional Record*, 90th Cong., 1st sess., August 2, 1967, 21094.
5. *Congressional Record*, 90th Cong., 1st sess., August 3, 1967, 21197.
6. *Congressional Record*, 90th Cong., 1st sess., August 2, 1967, 21087.

own congressional district, I hear talk about the decline of respect for the law. People talk about the "good old days" when kids were afraid to heckle the policeman on the beat; when kids had respect for the uniform of a cop; when kids recognized the authority of a policeman unless they wanted a few black and blue marks for their trouble.[7]

Also from the Republican side of the aisle came this comment by Representative Edward Hutchinson (Rep.) of Michigan: "Recently our struggle to keep the criminal element under control has been hobbled by judicial decision. . . . Criminal prosecutions are being obstructed by devices of form rather than substance—and these devices are being sustained by the highest Court in the land."[8] And a similar view came from Representative Robert A. Taft, Jr. (Rep.) of Ohio. "Apparently the majority of the members of the Supreme Court of America [*sic*] are more interested in protecting the lawless than they are interested in preserving law and order. . . . We need to stop certain members of the Federal judiciary in its all-out efforts to protect the criminals regardless of the crime committed."[9]

No amendments, however, were presented to overrule those certain members of the federal judiciary. The Senate was notified August 9, 1967, of the House passage of H.R. 5037.[10]

The Senate did not consider H.R. 5037 during 1967. Although during the hearings Senator McClellan had expressed the hope of having a bill passed during the summer of 1967, he was not able to get approval of his conglomerate S. 917 until late in the fall that year.[11]

7. *Congressional Record*, 90th Cong., 1st sess., August 3, 1967, 21198.
8. *Ibid.*, 21187, 21188.
9. *Ibid.*, 21197.
10. *Congressional Record*, 90th Cong., 1st sess., August 9, 1967 22040.
11. The committee bill contained the following titles: Title I. *Law Enforcement Assistance*, providing for planning grants, grants for law enforcement purposes, financial support for training, education, research, demonstration, and special purposes; Title II. *Admissibility of*

The Senate leadership called up S. 917 for debate on May 1, 1968, more than nine months after the hearings were concluded. Senator McClellan managed the committee bill and it was clear that the debate would be sharp on the portions of the bill added to the administration bill by the subcommittee. McClellan stated:

> No matter how much money we appropriate for local police departments, we will not have effective law enforcement so long as the courts allow self-confessed criminals to go unpunished. The confusion and disarray injected into law enforcement by such decisions as *Mallory* . . . *Escobedo* . . . and *Miranda* . . . are deplorable and demoralizing. They have weakened intolerably the force and effect of our criminal laws, and Congress had better do something about it.[12]

It should be recalled that *Mallory* turned on Rule 5(a) of the Federal Rules of Criminal Procedure which requires an arrested person to be brought before a committing magistrate without *unnecessary* delay. Since it was merely a "rule" it could be altered by legislation—so ran the argument by those endorsing that section of Title II. Interestingly, Senator McClellan quoted Warren Burger, then on the District of Columbia Court of Appeals. Justice Burger had dissented in a case in which the majority applied the *Mallory* rule. "It is inconceivable to me," Burger said, "that justice would go to such lengths ignoring a reasonable balance between individual rights and the protection of the public."[13] McClellan reserved some of his scorn for judicial pronouncements by referring to

---

Confessions, Reviewability in Admission in Evidence of Confessions in State Cases, Admissibility in Evidence of Eye Witness Testimony, and Procedures in Obtaining Writs of Habeas Corpus; Title III. *Wiretapping and Electronic Surveillance;* Title IV. *State Firearms Control Assistance Findings and Declaration; and* Title V. *General Provisions.* The president's proposals were reflected in Title I with a number of modifications.

12. *Congressional Record*, 90th Cong., 2nd sess., May 1, 1968, 11201.
13. *Killough* v. *U.S.*, 315 F. 2d 241, decided October 4, 1963.

the *Alston* case, also from the U.S. Court of Appeals for the District of Columbia.[14]

But the acme of irrationality and the ultimate in absurdity occurred when the same U.S. Court of Appeals . . . reversed the manslaughter conviction of Tom E. Alston, Jr., because he was interviewed for 5 minutes before being taken to a magistrate for arraignment. . . . This is the age of change. It is time for change—time for change in the Supreme Court of the United States. The thrust of the Miranda ruling, if it is not changed, will sweep us into the throes of anarchy and horror.[15]

McClellan and his supporters wanted to allow interrogation of an arrested person and give the police time to do it, and also to allow the trial court to determine whether a confession was voluntary. Even though opponents of this view cited cases of trial judges admitting confessions in evidence not voluntarily given and where abuses accompanied the extraction of admissions of guilt, the mood of the Senate was to enact legislation allowing a return to "what have been the law in practically every State and in all Federal Circuits."[16]

McClellan next focused attention on the claimed effects of the *Wade* decision.[17]

. . . the court held that an identifying witnesses' participation in a post indictment pretrial lineup without notice to and in absence of the accused's counsel denies him the right to counsel and calls into question the admissibility at the trial of the in-court identification of the accused witnesses who attended the lineup. . . . Section 3503 would simply deny jurisdiction to the Supreme Court or any inferior Federal court established by Congress to modify the ruling of any Federal or State trial court admitting in evidence in any criminal prosecution the testimony of a witness that he saw the accused commit or participate in the commission of a crime for which the accused is tried. . . .

14. *Alston* v. *U.S.*, 348 F. 2d 72 (1965).
15. *Congressional Record*, 90th Cong., 2nd sess., May 1, 1968, 11202.
16. In his opening remarks Senator McClellan said that if he were in sympathy with criminals he would vote against Title II.
17. *Congressional Record*, 90th Cong., 2nd sess., May 1, 1968, 11207.

As stated in chapter four, reference was frequently made by witnesses during the hearings to the split decisions of the Supreme Court, especially five to four decisions. Dissenting opinions were often the base from which arguments were made. In *Miranda*, for example, Justice Clark, in his dissent, wrote: "The Court further holds that failure to follow the new procedures requires inexorably the exclusion of any statement of the accused, as well as the fruits thereof. Such a strict constitutional specific inserted at the nerve center of crime detection may well kill the patient." [18]

In his dissent, Justice Harlan said:

> Society has always paid a stiff price for law and order, and peaceful interrogation is not one of the dark moments of the law. . . . Nothing in the letter or the spirit of the Constitution or in the precedents squares with the heavy-handed and one-sided action that is so precipitously taken by the Court in the name of fulfilling its constitutional responsibilities. [19]

And in his dissent, Justice White wrote:

> There is, in my view, every reason to believe that a good many criminal defendants, who otherwise would have been convicted on what this Court has previously thought to be the most satisfactory kind of evidence, will now, under this new version of the fifth amendment, either not be tried at all or acquitted if the State's evidence, minus the confession, is put to the test of litigation. I have no desire whatsoever to share the responsibility for any such impact on the present criminal process. [20]

Senator Tydings was the floor manager for the opponents of Title II. Periodically during the Senate debate, Tydings included in the *Congressional Record* letters he had received (at his invitation) from legal scholars, law schools, and law deans

18. 384 U.S. 436, 500.
19. *Ibid.*, 504, 505.
20. *Ibid.*, 542.

—all opposing Title II. But as indicated elsewhere, these opponents were noticeably absent among those testifying at the Senate subcommittee hearings.[21]

In his opening remarks, Tydings pointedly agreed with the proponents of Title II that the obvious purpose of the title was to try to overrule some Supreme Court decisions. It was quite obvious, he said, that the provisions denied appellate jurisdiction to the federal courts. Senator Wayne Morse (Dem.) of Oregon, while agreeing with the announced intent of the title was more concerned with the substance of the proposal.

> . . . in my judgment, the Supreme Court was not only right but the decisions are also precious to the perpetuation of the civil liberties and the freedom of the American people. . . . Do not forget that our whole system of criminal jurisprudence is based upon the presumption of innocence, the old Anglo-Saxon requirement that the State must establish guilt and not the arrested party his innocence. The presumption applies to the guilty as well as to the innocent. That is one of the principal ways we maintain in a free society a system of government by law rather than a government by police duress. . . . I am shocked by the bill in what it would do to free men in a supposedly free society, if it becomes the law of the land. Once again, I warn the American people, "Do not let the crisis of the hour cause us to create a greater crisis. A greater crisis to free society would be the denial of the precious civil and constitutional rights of free people." [22]

Proponents of Title II generally ignored the question of constitutionality, but opponents used every opportunity to disclaim it on that ground. Morse said:

> When it comes to a judiciable issue, and especially one of personal guarantees or due process of law in court proceedings, it is the courts that decide—not the Congress, not the President. . . . we find . . . sections that withdraw

21. Subcommittee chairman McClellan held firm control over the schedule of witnesses.

22. *Congressional Record*, 90th Cong., 2nd sess., May 2, 1968, 11594, 11595.

jurisdiction over several of these issues from the Federal courts. I must say that I find these the most repugnant sections of the whole bill.[23]

Frequently during the debate, opponents of Title II urged that those who wished to modify the effect of the rulings in *Mallory, Miranda,* or *Wade* do so by "proposing a new version of the fifth and sixth amendments that will eliminate the requirement of counsel at the lineup and eliminate the necessity for prompt arraignment of an accused person, and permit lengthy and indefinite police interrogation under conditions of isolation or any other conditions they wish to prescribe."[24] But these suggestions were ignored. At one point Morse said that it "smacks of a court-packing scheme: When you do not like the decision, change the judges. Or when you do not like the decision, withdraw the jurisdiction."[25] Again, proponents ignored the suggestion.

Senator McClellan's responses during the debate were similar to his statements during the hearings.

> . . . the crisis did not arise by reason of the quality of law enforcement we had under the old interpretation of the Constitution. . . . We had better law and order; we had better observance up to that time. It is the liberalization of the meaning of the Constitution today that is giving encouragement and a measure of protection to the violator. That is what we undertake to change by some of the provisions of the bill. We attempt to go back to the law and the Constitution as they were before the Court undertook to liberalize them to the point that today it is becoming almost a rule of the Court that it find some technicality to release back on society, habitual, confirmed, and confessed criminals.[26]

McClellan and his supporters repeatedly spoke of the "crisis" in law enforcement. Again and again they insisted

23. *Ibid.,* 11595.
24. *Ibid.,* 11596.
25. *Ibid.*
26. *Ibid.,* 11600.

that the U.S. courts were to blame for they, the courts, were bent on keeping criminals out of jail and able to continue to ply their trade. Proponents would not admit that the court decisions they attacked came from recognized abuses in the administration of justice. They argued, instead, that the methods of detection, apprehension, interrogation, and prosecution, procedural and substantive, were good and proper in the "old" days and if the nation could return to those days, the matter of having criminals loose would be rare indeed. Furthermore, freeing law enforcement officials from the interferences of the federal courts would mean the nation would be "safe for Americans." [27]

The rulings in *Miranda, Escobedo, Mallory, Wade*, and related cases did not make it "easy" for the police and prosecution. As Senator Edward W. Brooke (Rep.) of Massachusetts said during the debate on May 3, 1968, "The Miranda decision admittedly does not make life easier for the police. But in the long run the decision will result in improved law-enforcement procedure." [28]

Such views were not given support by opponents. Senator Bible said in response that "we enter this debate in a condition of outrage. The vast majority of Americans are fed up with what seems to be a pampering and mollycoddling of lawbreakers." [29]

Tydings sought to dispel the argument that the court decisions under attack were all recent. He cited especially *Brown* v. *Mississippi*, a 1935 case, which involved the voluntariness of a confession. The Supreme Court in that case said that merely "because a State may dispense with a jury trial, it does not follow that it may substitute trial by ordeal. The rack and torture chamber may not be substituted for the witness stand . . . and the use of the confessions thus obtained as the basis for conviction and sentence was a clear denial of due process." [30] Tydings also cited studies and surveys, saying

27. *Ibid.*, 11611.
28. *Congressional Record*, 90th Cong., 2nd sess., May 3, 1968, 11745.
29. *Ibid.*, 11754.
30. 297 U.S. 278, 285, 286.

of them that "all these agree that *Miranda* has changed almost nothing and that police are not really hampered in their activities by this decision." [31]

Tydings complained that there had been "no public hearings . . . in which law professors, students, or criminologists, had an opportunity to testify." [32] And Senator McClellan did not deny this; rather, however, he said the views of legal scholars were represented by the testimony of Charles E. Moyland, Jr., then state's attorney for the city of Baltimore! [33] That response came after Tydings indicated he had letters opposing Title II from 38 law schools, 206 legal scholars, and 21 law school deans.

Another argument advanced by opponents of Title II was the relationship among the three branches of government which would be impaired by its passage. Senator Fong (Rep.) of Hawaii noted that

> abolition of Supreme Court jurisdiction would seriously distort the delicate balance that is maintained between our three branches of Government. . . . An attempt by the Congress to abolish the traditional power of judicial review . . . would set an extremely bad precedent . . . since there would be nothing to prevent Congress from enacting similar legislation whenever the Court handed down a decision with which Congress disagreed. [34]

One aspect of the effect of Title II which troubled opponents was the elimination of any degree of uniformity among the states and the federal government in affected criminal procedures. Tydings observed, borrowing from Hamilton's *Federalist* No. 80, that "Title II carries Hamilton's example to

31. *Congressional Record*, 90th Cong., 2nd sess., May 6, 1968, 11896. See also, Richard J. Medalie, Leonard Zeitz, and Paul Alexander, "Custodial Police Interrogation in Our Nation's Capital: The Attempt to Implement Miranda," *Michigan Law Review* 66 no. 7 (May 1968): 1347–1422.

32. *Congressional Record*, 90th Cong., 2nd sess., May 6, 1968, 11901.

33. Senate Subcommittee *Hearings*, 1967, p. 619.

34. *Congressional Record*, 90th Cong., 2nd sess., May 8, 1968, 12293.

a nightmare extreme: a 50-headed hydra, with each State court having final jurisdiction in its State regarding confessions and eyewitness evidence." [35]

To offset any effect the law school letters might have, McClellan frequently received consent to include in the record letters he had received from numerous people in all walks of life, including police and prosecutors and judges, and also newspaper editorials. These supported his position for Title II.

Although debate was intermittent, Senate attendance small, and calls for a quorum frequent, by May 8, 1968, it was clear that the debate was becoming repetitive and would soon end. But on that day, and the day following two events helped shape the outcome.

On May 8, President Johnson wrote a letter to Senator Mike Mansfield (Dem.) of Montana, the majority floor leader, in which he urged the passage of his proposals submitted the year before. He did not mention Title II (or Title III on wire tapping), but it was clear that he was against those provisions, especially Title II. His letter, urging legislation to bring safety to the streets, contained these words: "We can do this best by: ... not encumbering the legislation with provisions raising grave constitutional questions and which might jeopardize the prompt passage of Title I." [36] This was the only announced evidence of support to the opponents of Title II. The Senate majority leadership outwardly at least did little or nothing.

On May 9, 1968, the day after the Johnson letter, Nixon headquarters released a statement entitled "Toward Freedom from Fear." It was Richard M. Nixon's position paper on crime, one of several position papers on a range of subjects issued during the preconvention period. In contrast to the president's indirect opposition to Title II, the Nixon statement was in strong support of Title II. It lashed out at the federal courts, especially the Supreme Court, for the decisions supporting the rulings in *Escobedo*, *Miranda*, and *Wade*. In the

35. *Congressional Record*, 90th Cong., 2nd sess., May 9, 1968, 12479.
36. *Ibid.*, 12450.

section of the statement entitled "Striking the Balance," Nixon stated:

> The balance must be shifted back toward the peace forces in our society and a requisite step is to redress the imbalance created by these specific court decisions. I would urge Congress to enact proposed legislation that—dealing with both Miranda and Escobedo—would leave it to the judge and the jury to determine both the voluntariness and the validity of any confession. The Miranda and Escobedo decisions of the high court have had the effect of seriously ham stringing the peace forces in our society and strengthening the criminal forces. And I think they point up a genuine need—a need for future presidents to include in their appointments to the United States Supreme Court men who are thoroughly experienced and versed in the criminal laws of the land.[37]

He also referred to Title II saying it should pass "despite the vigorous opposition of the Attorney General." He then said that the ruling in *Wade* should be cast aside by the Congress, indicating that having an attorney present at a police line-up was not necessary to insure a fair trial and doing so would not violate the right to counsel.[38]

The majority decision in *Miranda* contained the following:

> It is impossible for us to foresee the potential alternatives for protecting the privilege which might be devised by Congress or the States in the exercise of their creative rule-making capacities. Therefore we cannot say that the Constitution necessarily requires adherence to any particular solution for the inherent compulsions of the interrogation process as it is presently conducted. Our decision in no way creates a constitutional straitjacket which will handicap sound efforts at reform, nor is it intended to have this effect. *We encourage Congress and the States to con-*

37. *Congressional Record*, 90th Cong., 2nd sess., May 13, 1968, 12937, 12938.

38. It was probably mere coincidence that the Johnson letter and the Nixon statement came almost the same day, but the statement probably influenced some votes in the Senate.

tinue their laudable search for increasingly effective ways of pro-
tecting the rights of the individual while promoting efficient
enforcement of our criminal laws.[39]

Senator Hruska brought the above statement to the attention of the Senate, saying that "the Supreme Court invited
congressional consideration—invited action by Congress on
this subject—in an effort to try to make progress in this very
difficult field. . . . In light of the Court's invitation, we have
proceeded, and we are trying to make progress."[40]

No one could argue that promoting the efficiency of law
enforcement should be opposed, but it can be argued that
removing the appellate jurisdiction of the federal courts in
state cases is hardly in harmony with any "laudable search for
increasingly effective ways of protecting the rights of the
individual while promoting efficient enforcement of our
criminal laws."

Senator Stephen M. Young (Dem.) of Ohio claimed that
Title II would invite a return to "third degree police practices" and permit the use of confessions "no matter how
fictitious or erroneous the finding of the State court might
be."[41]

Senator McClellan found comfort, as did his supporters, in
the fact that four justices of the Supreme Court agreed with
him.

Thus, it is not a matter of a personal vendetta against the
Supreme Court, or of personal feeling. It is crucial to the
peace and tranquility of America. It is crucial to law enforcement. It is imperative that the current trends be
reversed. Law and order in America cannot be restored
unless we restore that procedure and that quality of
justice which prevailed in this country for so long which
kept down the crime rate.[42]

39. 384 U.S. 436, 467. (Emphasis supplied.)
40. *Congressional Record*, 90th Cong., 2nd sess., May 10, 1968,
12822.
41. *Congressional Record*, 90th Cong., 2nd sess., May 13, 1968,
12924.
42. *Ibid.*, 12964.

The debate in the Senate was scheduled to reach a crucial point when Tydings obtained agreement to vote on a motion to strike Title II in its entirety. He then offered a substitute:

> The Congress finds that extensive factual investigation of the actual impact on law enforcement of the decisions of the United States Supreme Court regarding criminal law procedure is a necessary prerequisite to legislative action pertaining to such decisions. The Congress therefore directs that the appropriate Committee or Committees of the Congress undertake such investigation of Court decisions before the Congress considers legislative action regarding them.[43]

Senator McClellan's response was prompt. Without Title II, he said, "No matter how much money we appropriate for local police departments we will not have effective law enforcement so long as the courts allow self-confessed criminals to go unpunished."[44]

By May 17, Senator Tydings had included 212 letters from legal scholars, 43 law schools, and 24 law deans—all opposing Title II. He also included in the *Congressional Record* a statement of the opposition to it from the Judicial Conference of the United States—except for the *Wade* ruling and that exception because the conference had not considered it. Earlier, Senator McClellan had cited support of Title II by the National District Attorneys Association. Senator Tydings countered by including a statement of opposition by the Criminal Law Section of the American Bar Association, and the American Law Institute. This led Senator Russell B. Long (Dem.) of Louisiana, to question, he said, a learned judge who told him: "Senator, can't you figure that out? Do you know who is the criminal section of the American Bar Association? Those are the lawyers who defend criminals. Don't you realize that if crime has increased by 400 percent, their income has increased by 400 percent?"[45]

43. *Congressional Record*, 90th Cong., 2nd sess., May 17, 1968, 13830.

44. *Ibid.*, 13845.

45. *Congressional Record*, 90th Cong., 2nd sess., May 20, 1968, 14028.

As the general debate was about to end, Senator Brooke observed:

> It is very curious to me that the *Miranda* case can be condemned in some quarters as being itself responsible for the rising crime rate, when it merely calls for procedures similar to those adopted voluntarily years earlier by the Federal Bureau of Investigation. . . . we are threatened with double standards of justice . . . ours is an "accusitorial" not an "inquisitorial" system.[46]

On May 21, 1968, three weeks after Senate consideration began, a combination of Republicans and southern Democrats rejected the Tydings substitute. The vote was thirty-one to fifty-one. Only seven Republicans and one southern Democrat (Ralph Yarborough of Texas) supported the move to kill Title II. The Republicans were George D. Aiken of Vermont, J. Caleb Boggs of Delaware, Edward W. Brooke of Massachusetts, Clifford P. Case of New Jersey, John Sherman Cooper of Kentucky, Hiram L. Fong of Hawaii, and Charles H. Percy of Illinois.

Had it been adopted, the Tydings substitute for Title II would have eliminated the overrule efforts being pursued by Senator McClellan. It would presumably have meant that the House and Senate Committees on the Judiciary would have had to begin a lengthy excursion into the decisions of the federal appellate courts and the U.S. Supreme Court. It could also have meant an examination of many state practices. Tydings had appealed to the Senate membership saying that there was no empirical evidence to show that the Court rulings had really had an adverse impact. But whether the majority who voted to keep Title II did not relish the prospect of the inquiry or whether they thought it might disprove their case is not known. It seemed at the time that the sponsors of the Senate version of S. 917, Title II, wanted to serve notice on the federal courts that the mood was quite strong, even bitter, about the recent rulings, and they were going to be reversed one way or another.

46. *Congressional Record*, 90th Cong., 2nd sess., May 21, 1968, 14134.

Some of the proponents of Title II also may have thought that by eliminating the section intended to curtail the appellate jurisdiction of the federal courts—then known to have strong opposition—the Supreme Court might accept the provisions relating to interrogation, confessions, and arraignment. Although not publicly stated it can be assumed that the entire Senate membership believed that it would not be long before changes in the personnel of the Supreme Court might bring about reversals of the hated decisions or at least modify them enough to make them more palatable. As the votes were taken in May, President Johnson had already announced his decision not to be a candidate for another term, and before the deadline was reached for the president's signing of the bill, Chief Justice Warren had indicated he would soon retire from the Court. Warren had written the opinions in both *Brown* (the school desegregation case) and *Miranda,* and the southern Senators did not need to be reminded of it.

The next stage was a vote of twenty-nine to fifty-five defeating an effort to delete the provisions which were aimed at overturning the ruling in *Miranda.*[47] Next, by a vote of twenty-six to fifty-eight the Senate rejected efforts to eliminate those provisions intended to overrule the decision in *Mallory.*[48]

As reported by the Committee on the Judiciary, Title II carried no limit on the time interrogation would be allowable without having any resulting statement or confession unrestricted as evidence in a trial. Senator Scott offered an amendment to provide for a four-hour delay before arraignment—interrogation time—but he asked that his amendment be changed to provide six hours. He said he preferred three or four hours and also referred to the 1967 statute for the District of Columbia which allowed three hours, "but I am striving here for the art of the possible, and in trying to accommodate the views of a number of Senators, have come up with 6 hours, for the purpose of allowing time for out-of-state checks follow-

47. Except for the six-hour rule adopted later, the section was the same as reported to the Senate by the Committee on the Judiciary.
48. *Congressional Record,* 90th Cong., 2nd sess., May 21, 1968, 14174.

ing the apprehension of the person charged with the crime."[49] Senator McClellan indicated he would agree to the six hours. He would not agree to a plea from Senator Tydings that it be made three hours since the Congress concluded three hours was acceptable only a few months before in the District of Columbia statute. Anyway, McClellan insisted, he was making quite a concession to having a stated time limit since the committee bill did not carry one.

On a voice vote, the six-hour provision was accepted. This voice vote was the only one so taken on the crucial votes. All others were on roll call. The voice vote was taken, however, because of an earlier agreement that no further roll calls would be taken that day after the preceding one. Apparently no effort was made by the majority leadership to delay a vote until the following day or to endeavor to gain support against the six-hour provision. Presumably it did not because the president the previous year had approved the bill for the District of Columbia. There is no record of how many Senators voiced their support for the six-hour feature.

The next roll call vote was crucial for both sides. At the heart of Title II was the denial of appellate jurisdiction to the federal courts of state cases. Earlier Senator Scott said during general debate that he could not support that provision.[50] Senator Albert Gore (Dem.) of Tennessee briefly discussed the provision and indicated his opposition. He said, "I submit . . . that this goes too far, and I cannot support it. . . . I do not wish to deny to the Federal courts, nor do I wish to deny to an American citizen, the reviewability by the Federal courts of a constitutional right which he thinks may have been infringed."[51]

But Senator Ervin complained that if the section were eliminated the Senate would be most inconsistent.

49. Public Law 90-226 was signed by President Johnson on December 27, 1967. It authorized police in the district to make warrantless arrests for certain offenses and provided for a three-hour investigative detention. This was the first successful effort by the Congress to soften the effects of *Mallory*.

50. *Congressional Record*, 90th Cong., 2nd sess., May 21, 1968, 14140.

51. *Ibid.*, 14175.

Congress has no power to prescribe procedures in State courts; and this is the only way in which the Senate can restore to the State courts the power to convict, on voluntary confessions, self-confessed murderers, self-confessed rapists, self-confessed robbers, self-confessed arsonists, and self-confessed thieves in cases where the newly invented rule in the Miranda case was not followed by the law enforcement officer having them in custody.[52]

The hard core of the Republican–southern Democrat bloc held firm. Thirty-two voted to deny appellate jurisdiction.[53] They lost, however, with fifty-two Senators unwilling to curtail the Court's jurisdiction.[54]

Next, by a vote of twenty-one to sixty-three, section 3502 was approved. It related to the ruling in *Wade* on eyewitness testimony, but by a vote of fifty-one to thirty, the Senate dropped the restriction on the appellate jurisdiction of the federal courts in state cases. Presumably the vote on the prior section predicted the outcome.

Thus, for all practical purposes, S. 917, Title II, was approved as it affected *Mallory*, *Miranda*, and *Wade*. The Senate had served its notice of its displeasure and opposition about these rulings, but it did not find it acceptable to do what Senators McClellan and Ervin urged that they do, namely to curtail the appellate jurisdiction of the federal courts and its power to review state cases. Whether many Senators had familiarized themselves with Supreme Court opinions on the power of Congress to regulate its jurisdiction in appellate matters is not known. Senator Tydings mentioned the case of *Ex parte McCardle* and other cases[55] bearing on the subject. In *McCardle*, Chief Justice Salmon P. Chase stated that the appellate jurisdiction of the Supreme Court came from the Constitution, not from legislation, but that the Constitution gave the Congress power to make exceptions. The provision reads: "In all other cases before mentioned, the Supreme

52. *Ibid.*, 14176.
53. *Ibid.*, 14177.
54. *Ibid.*
55. 7 Wallace 506 (1868). *McCardle* and related cases will be considered in chapter six.

Court shall have appellate Jurisdiction, both as to Law and Fact, with such Exceptions, and under such regulations as the Congress shall make." [56] It may long be debated whether the exceptions being made in proposed Title II were the kind the Supreme Court would tolerate.

Title II contained a section unrelated to the Court rulings under attack. Section 2256 was intended to severely restrict the use of the writ of habeas corpus by the federal courts in state cases. No proposal like it was in the form of a bill before the subcommittee during the 1967 hearings, but reference was made to the use of the writ by Judge Homer L. Kreider of the Court of Common Pleas, Harrisburg, Pennsylvania. He also arranged to have a statement by a former president of the Pennsylvania Bar Association included which discussed "the deplorable situation resulting from the wholesale abuse of habeas corpus by the filing of frivolous and repetitive petitions." The use of the writ, it was claimed by the judges, in increasing numbers resulted from the U.S. Supreme Court decision in *Fay* v. *Noia*[57] and *Townsend* v. *Sain*[58] in which the Court "liberalized the use of the Federal habeas corpus procedure to such an extent that it is now being used as a substitute for direct appeal." [59] It was also claimed to have so increased the caseload of the courts that it was disrupting the orderly process of the final disposition of state criminal cases.[60] Judge W. Walter Braham told the bar association on January 19, 1967, that "no sooner were the decisions of the Supreme Court which we have cited released than word about them flashed through the dim, occult reaches of the penitentiaries, and the courts have been flooded with habeas corpus cases ever since." He claimed that about 30 percent of the business of the federal courts "derives from habeas corpus." [61]

56. Article III, sec. 2.
57. 372 U.S. 391 (1963).
58. 372 U.S. 293 (1963).
59. Report no. 1097 to accompany S. 917, p. 63 (cited above p. 77 n. 15).
60. *Ibid.*
61. Senate Subcommittee *Hearings*, 1967, pp. 278, 280.

A statement from Judge James S. Bowman of the Court of Common Pleas of Dauphin County, Pennsylvania, urged congressional action "to proscribe the use of the Federal courts" in that manner.[62]

The report to accompany S. 917 carried only brief mention of the above testimony, but it was considered significant enough by its sponsors to make it a special section and restrict the use of the writ.[63] On May 21, 1968, it came up for vote as one of the several divisions taken that day. Senator Tydings urged its elimination, indicating that to deny the writ would not do what the proponents wanted, that is, prevent the U.S. Supreme Court or other appellate federal courts from hearing appeals on constitutional questions by convicted persons. The writ of certiorari would still be available, but the route would be a long one. Senator Ervin replied that the provision was in the bill because the chief justices of the states had asked for it.[64]

Senator Brooke observed rhetorically that "is it not true that the writ of habeas corpus is the only guarantee that a defendant in a State proceeding who has a constitutional question will have that question decided upon by the Federal judiciary?"[65] Tydings replied, "That is true. It is true because only writ of certiorari to the Supreme Court would be left for Federal review. This would put an impossible burden on the Supreme Court."[66]

After appeals to preserve the current use of the writ, Senator Scott brought the discussion to a near conclusion saying, "Mr. President, it is my feeling that while I voted to keep other sections of title II, if Congress tampers with the great writ, its actions would have about as much chance of being held constitutional as the celebrated celluloid dog chasing the asbestos cat through hell."[67]

62. *Ibid.*, p. 290.
63. Section 2256 of Title II.
64. *Congressional Record*, 90th Cong., 2nd sess., May 21, 1968, 14182.
65. *Ibid.*, 14183.
66. *Ibid.*
67. *Ibid.*

A division produced fifty-four to strike the restriction from the bill. Twenty-seven wanted to retain it. Again the Republican–southern Democratic bloc showed its strength and it lost only three votes from the group which was unsuccessful in trying to curb the appellate review of the federal courts. Senator Robert C. Byrd of West Virginia, Senator Howard W. Cannon (Dem.) of Nevada, and Senator Norris Cotton (Rep.) of New Hampshire joined the majority to strike section 2256.[68]

Final Senate action came on May 23, 1968. By a vote of seventy-two to four the crime bill passed.[69]

The House of Representatives had passed H.R. 5037 the year before, on August 8. But even with many modifications it was the administration bill only. As the House considered the Senate's action, the immediate question was whether to call for a conference. Representative Celler on May 29, 1968, moved to disagree with the Senate version. But with brief debate the House agreed with the Senate! On June 5, Celler said of the Senate bill:

> . . . the U.S. Senate approved an illusory statute purportedly designed to control and prevent crime. In its present form, this measure is a cruel hoax on citizens for whom crime and the fear of crime are the facts of life. . . . It is built on false premises. Its provisions are illusory. It is destructive of the tenets of our liberty. . . . Unfortunately, at the present time our nation is encapsulated in fear. We have heard that to him who fears everything restless— and when fear enters—reason departs. This bill was adopted through fear.[70]

68. Senator Robert P. Griffin (Rep.) of Michigan said he found the proposal a very "drastic step" and urged its defeat.

69. After the vote Senator Mansfield said: ". . . with a loud and clear voice the Senate has said let us reverse the growing crime rate, let us give our law-enforcement officers the help and assistance they need. . . . With the passage of this measure the Senate has responded. I think this entire body may be proud of such an immense achievement." Senator Ervin, in praising Senator Tydings, said, "He and I disagreed on a few aspects of the bill, but he certainly merits the thanks of the country for the fine work he has done."

70. *Congressional Record*, 90th Cong., 2nd sess., June 5, 1968, 16066.

Representative Celler urged a conference, insisting that

> in this constitutional contest the Congress cannot be the
> winner. The Supreme Court will undoubtedly declare the
> very provisions of Title II unconstitutional. You have two
> remedies, neither of which you will assume. You could
> impeach the Justices, if you wished to get new Justices.
> . . . Second you could pack the court.[71]

But this was June 5, 1968. Senator Robert F. Kennedy had
been fatally wounded. The mood of the House was against
Representative Celler's plea. Instead, it possessed the mood
and attitude of Representative Ford, the minority leader:

> I refuse to concede, Mr. Speaker, that the elected repre-
> sentatives of the American people cannot be the winner
> in a confrontation with the U.S. Supreme Court. To
> admit that is to admit that the American people cannot
> control the U.S. Supreme Court . . . Let this vote today be
> the battleground.[72]

The vote was not even close. It was 317 to 60 against a
conference. Even the majority leader, Representative Carl
Albert (Dem.) of Oklahoma, and his whip, Representative
Hale Boggs (Dem.) of Louisiana, voted against calling a conference. The finale came with a vote of 369 to 17 for accepting
in toto the Senate version.

President Johnson signed the measure on June 19, the last
day he could have vetoed it. He was urged to veto it by the
American Civil Liberties Union and a number of members of
the Congress, but in approving it he merely said that some of
its features were unwise.[73]

71. *Ibid.*, 16069.
72. *Ibid.*, 16073, 16074.
73. Many members of the Congress up for re-election believed that
a "law and order" bill was necessary for their political survival.
They hoped that some of the objectionable features of the crime act
would later be changed. Supporters of Title II and III believed the
president wanted the provisions of Title I so much that he would have
no choice but to approve it. Senator McClellan had supported the
president for direct financial aid to local governments even though
block grants to the states prevailed in the final version.

VI

Conclusions: An Appraisal

Title II of the Omnibus Crime Act of 1968 is in conflict with the decision in *Miranda*. The majority in that decision did not say that voluntariness of a statement or confession was one of the standards to be followed. What *Miranda* did was to prescribe standards to determine whether a confession was indeed voluntarily given. The decision does not endorse the totality of circumstances as is authorized in Title II. The trial judge, to be sure, is to take four points into consideration, but they appear not to be all the points the judge might consider. The words are that the trial judge "in determining the issue of voluntariness shall take into consideration *all* the circumstances surrounding the giving of the confession, *including*" the points listed.[1] Can it not be assumed that "all" means everything which might bear on the question of voluntariness and "including" refers to those specified? This would have been clearer if the words "but not necessarily limited to" followed the word "included." As enacted it does not seem to rule out any other factors the trial judge might consider.

The rule in *Miranda* is that a suspect who is taken into custody or otherwise deprived of his freedom by the authorities in any significant way and is subjected to questioning must be advised *prior* to any questioning that he has a right to remain silent, that anything he says can be used against him in a court of law, that he has the right to the presence of an

1. Emphasis supplied.

attorney, and that if he cannot afford an attorney one will be appointed for him prior to any questioning if he so desires. Opportunity to exercise these rights must be afforded to him throughout any interrogation.[2]

It is true that the majority opinion in *Miranda* invited possible legislative action, but Title II is not in harmony with the safeguards announced in that case: that the safeguards be "fully as effective" as those prescribed. And the opinion also had this to say: "Where rights secured by the Constitution are involved, there can be no rule-making or legislation which would abrogate them."[3]

How, then, could the provisions of Title II be considered as effective as those in *Miranda?* The plain answer is that they cannot. A confession not meeting the criteria in *Miranda* would not be deemed as voluntarily given if those criteria were lessened. Presumably the requirements in *Miranda* involve rights "secured by the Constitution" or they would not be specified. Title II permits the trial judge to take circumstances into consideration, but the "presence or absence" of *any* of them need not be conclusive on the issue of whether a confession was given voluntarily.

There was no doubt that Senators McClellan and Ervin wanted a return to pre-*Miranda* practices and they sought to get it by giving the trial judge discretion.[4] He was authorized

2. During the hearings in June, 1968, on the separation of powers dealing with the U.S. Supreme Court, Senator Ervin, a member of the subcommittee, made this comment about *Miranda:* " *Miranda* was based upon a factual assumption, namely that law-enforcement officers in the United States are so bent on procuring convictions of people they arrest that they can't be trusted to interrogate them as they were for the first 166 years after the self-incrimination clause was put into the Constitution. . . . A decision of the Supreme Court, if it is based on a factual assumption which is incorrect, may be subject to Congress' power to legislate."

3. 384 U.S. 436, 490.

4. Many associates of Senators McClellan and Ervin believe that both men sincerely thought the Court decisions were wrong, had to be altered, and urgently so for society's safety and security. They insist these two Senators were not anticourt and were trying to find con-

choices, those listed, and others he might consider warranted. The Senators sought time for prearraignment interrogation before counsel might be present and in effect silence an accused from possible self-incrimination. Title II allows a maximum of six hours, plus added but unspecified time needed for travel to get to the nearest magistrate. Section 3501 requires that a confession, if admitted, be found voluntary, but if the time limits were exceeded, then voluntarily given or not, would the confession be considered involuntarily given? We do not know what a reasonable time lapse for travel would be, whether carefully within normal driving limits, or at the maximum speeds allowed by law, and we do not know whether the conversation en route would be solely about spectator sports.

What incensed so many police, prosecutors, and judges and some members of the Senate subcommittee were reported extremes such as one related by Judge Alexander Holtzoff of the District Court for the District of Columbia.

> The defendant was brought to police headquarters at 5:30 A.M. He was questioned by the police for about 5 minutes and then immediately confessed on the advice of his wife who had accompanied him with the police. It was held by the court of appeals that the arresting officers should have taken the defendant before a committing magistrate immediately and that the questioning, even for 5 minutes, was not permissible—and the conviction was reversed.[5]

The rule in *Mallory* was that arraignment be without unnecessary delay, and this was based on Rule 5(a) of the Federal Rules of Criminal Procedure. Proponents of Title II argued that since *Mallory* was based only on a rule, Congress

stitutional means to effect the changes they sought. Although not emphasized in the hearings, it has been suggested that the circumstances surrounding the use of the confession in *Miranda* could have been sanctioned as being "harmless error." See *Dickinson Law Review*, Spring 1968, no. 3, pp. 536–42.

5. Senate Subcommittee, *Hearings, 1967*, p. 260.

could change it. Section 3501(c) authorizes the six-hour rule and does indeed change it, for six hours is hardly prompt or without unnecessary delay. That does not necessarily mean, however, that the Supreme Court would automatically overrule that section. It would depend upon what constitutional rights were involved during the six hours, plus travel time, if any. If this assumption is correct, then the prescription in *Mallory* would have little consequence and section 3501(c) would survive.[6]

In *Wade* the rule was that a suspect in a police line-up

6. In one of his last opinions as circuit judge for the U.S. Court of Appeals, Warren Burger said that the standing of *Mallory* "has been drawn into serious doubt by recent Congressional enactments" and that it "is unsound to treat *Mallory* and *Miranda* as closely related; the former is a quantitive test of time delay, the latter is a qualitative test of the circumstances of the interrogation." He also said that "*Mallory* has never been interpreted as requiring the police to terminate an interview for purposes of arraignment when a suspect wants to make a confession of guilt." *Frazier* v. *U.S.*, decided March 14, 1969.

In a memorandum issued June 11, 1969, the U.S. Department of Justice issued a statement to all United States attorneys on the subject of Title II. It stated in part:

> Aside from any constitutional issues, therefore, it is impossible to predict how much weight a particular court will give to the absence of any one of the factors mentioned. For this reason, the only safe course for federal investigative agents, and for such United States Attorneys as may have occasion to talk with defendants, is to continue their present practice of giving the full *Miranda* warnings.
> The area where we believe the statute can be effective and where a legislative constitutional argument can be made is the situation where a voluntary confession is obtained after less than perfect warning or less than conclusive waiver, as, for example, where an agent inadvertently fails to fully explain the right to have counsel appointed for an indigent, or a written waiver is not obtained. The admissibility of the confession may be urged in an argument framed along the following lines:
> In *Miranda* v. *Arizona*, 384 U.S. 439, the Supreme Court stated that confessions by persons accused of crime were "a proper element in law enforcement" and that "[a]ny statement given freely and voluntarily without any compelling influences is, of course, admissible in evidence." 384 U.S. at 478. The Court found, however, that persons in police custody are, by virtue of

identified by a witness could not have that identification confirmed in a trial unless counsel for the accused was present if he so desired. *Wade* did not exclude eyewitness testimony. But section 3502 of Title II appears to give unqualified use of eyewitness testimony and without regard to time, place, or circumstance. It is a clear authorization. It does not mention the accused's right to counsel at a police line-up, and whether it happens frequently or not there is evidence that those selected for line-ups are of such variety that an eyewitness would have little difficulty in identifying some suspects and the guilty ones.[7]

------

that custody alone, subject to a form of "compulsion inherent in custodial surroundings." *Id.*, at 458; see *Id.*, 465, 467, 478. In order to dispel this inherent compulsion and thus to safeguard the individual's Fifth Amendment right "to remain silent unless he chooses to speak in the unfettered exercise of his own will" (*id.*, at 460), the Court held that accused persons must be made aware of their "right of silence" and assured a "continuous opportunity to exercise it." *Id.*, at 444; see *id.*, at 467, 479, 490....

Since those specific warnings are not themselves constitutionally absolute, the determination by Congress—that their absence in a case should not entail an inflexible imposition of the exclusionary rule—is within the power of Congress....

In short, while the Court in *Miranda* tried to set forth a set of rules which would avoid the necessity of considering all the circumstances of a particular case, Congress has, in effect, told the courts that it does want the cases considered on an individual basis....

Reprinted in the *Congressional Record*, 91st Cong., 1st sess., August 11, 1969, daily edition, S 9567, 9568.

7. In *Stovall* v. *Denno*, 388 U.S. 293, decided June 12, 1967, the Supreme Court upheld as valid a line-up in which the defendant was the only Negro present. In the Department of Justice memorandum cited above, p. 98 n. 6, the following was stated: "In our view, Section 3502 can constitutionally be read as directed to the collateral rule of evidence under which the government must show by 'clear and convincing' evidence that, where a pretrial identification occurred without an opportunity for counsel or other safeguards, a proposed in-court identification by a witness is based upon observations of the suspect other than the pretrial identification proceeding." *Wade* might give way because it was a new requirement and because of a belief that the Congress is as knowledgeable as the Supreme Court on the subject.

Title II refers to criminal prosecutions only in federal courts. It leaves unanswered the problem of possible dual systems of justice, one for the federal courts and something else for the state courts. Apparently Senators McClellan and Ervin wanted the rules to be similar as long as the decisions of the trial judges were followed, and in state cases if the highest tribunal (appellate) affirmed the voluntariness of a confession used in evidence. Supporters of this position argued that the states were quite capable of handling matters of that kind because the trial judge and jury dealt with the question first hand. They were in a far better position, it was claimed, to determine fairness than any review court especially any federal court. But with the provisions of Title II applicable only to federal cases, what happens to *Miranda*, *Mallory*, and *Wade* as they apply to state trials? Nothing in the legislation has changed their status in state cases so they must be still in effect—although the six-hour rule might find acceptance since it was countering a rule. If true, then there are two different standards. On the other hand, if the McClellan-Ervin provisions denying appellate jurisdiction to the federal courts in state cases had been enacted, the possibility could have been to have one set of provisions for federal cases and as many as fifty standards for the states, each state being freed from possible federal review.

Two different sets of rules were denounced in *Gideon* and *Malloy*. The U.S. Supreme Court said in *Pointer* v. *Texas*,[8] two years after *Gideon*, that "it can no longer broadly be said that the Sixth Amendment does not apply to state courts." In *Malloy* v. *Hogan*[9] the Court said that like the guarantee against self-incrimination, the Sixth Amendment was "to be enforced against the States under the Fourteenth Amendment according to the same standards that protect those rights against federal encroachment." In *Murphy* v. *Waterfront Commission*[10] the Court affirmed its position that there had to be the same standards in state and federal courts on the immunity of a

8. 380 U.S. 400 (1965).
9. 378 U.S. 1 (1964).
10. 378 U.S. 52 (1964).

witness for testimony which might incriminate him. The same standards must determine whether silence in either a federal or state proceeding is justified. The privilege against self-incrimination protects a state witness against federal prosecution.[11]

Senator Ervin observed during the hearings that the Congress had the power to define the substance of due process and matters of self-incrimination for the states. He said that section 5 of the Fourteenth Amendment gave the Congress authority to enforce the provisions of the amendment by appropriate legislation. To him that meant the Congress could define due process for the states and the courts could not do anything about it. This suggestion was a part of his effort to find a way, short of constitutional amendment, to restrict the appellate jurisdiction of the federal courts of state trials, and especially the U.S. Supreme Court.

Evidence used in a trial must have been legally obtained. But one bill before the Senate subcommittee was intended to alter existing rules as the U.S. Supreme Court applied them to state courts. A flexible rule was suggested in the bill to give the trial judge discretion whether evidence seized by unreasonable search and seizure could be admitted in evidence. This bill was opposed by the U.S. Attorney General, but this may not have been the reason it was not reported out of committee.[12]

Presumably members of the committee were unwilling to adopt the English practice of admitting evidence no matter how obtained if it was relevant to the case. Under certain conditions that practice was for a time acceptable under the so-called "silver platter" doctrine wherein state officers could seize evidence and give it over to federal authorities who in turn would use it legally in federal courts because they had no part in obtaining it in the first instance. This cooperative effort was set aside by the U.S. Supreme Court in *Elkins* v. *U.S.*[13] That decision is but another instance of the position

11. Citing *Malloy* v. *Hogan*, 378 U.S. 1 (1964).
12. See Senate Subcommittee, *Hearings, 1967*, pp. 109, 110.
13. 364 U.S. 206 (1960).

taken by the high court denying two standards. Accepting the lesser standards for federal trials and something more restrictive for state cases seems unlikely. The question remains what will happen if the states begin to adopt the provisions of Title II. Even if section 3501 is upheld, it is difficult to believe that the federal appellate courts, especially the U.S. Supreme Court, will disavow its supervisory role over the proceedings of the trial courts.

What the Senate did not do in Title II as a result of floor amendments is significant. Even though the requirement in *Mallory* was substantially altered with the six-hour rule, the categoric allowance for eyewitness testimony affecting *Wade* sustained, and the *Miranda* standards challenged by alternatives, these changes made the measure applicable only to the federal courts. It can be argued that even these provisions would not have been so overwhelmingly approved were it not that members of the Congress and the president became familiar with the problem of crime in the District of Columbia. They are quite near it.[14]

During the hearings several witnesses compared the procedures followed by the FBI and which were mentioned approvingly by Chief Justice Warren in *Miranda*. They noted that the agency had followed the requirements being announced in Miranda and that it had compiled a good record. Warren said it was "an exemplary record of effective law enforcement."[15] One witness responded to the comparisons between the FBI and local law enforcement agencies in this way:

> But the distinction between the responsibility of local police and the FBI is a very substantial one. The FBI, generally speaking, deals with the more sophisticated type of crime. . . . But unlike our local police, the FBI does not enter the area of the day-by-day street crimes such as muggings, and rapes, and robberies. And furthermore, there is an obligation imposed upon our local police to prevent crime, and that is where the *Miranda*

14. The district, of course, serves as a unit of local government.
15. Senate Subcommittee, *Hearings, 1967,* p. 40.

rule has a great impact on the prevention of crime, and the FBI is not charged with that responsibility.[16]

And an investigator for Anoka County, Minnesota, gave this reaction:

> Another problem with *Miranda* is that if a constable or untrained officer in a small village some distance away, should pick up someone and question the party about a crime in our jurisdiction without giving the *Miranda* warning and the party makes certain admissions, believe me this case is blown out the window. So along this line where there are communities that do not have funds to train officers there should be some type of State or Federal funds to assure that this is done. Decisions from the Supreme Court are coming down so fast that in a department a size of ours where we only have sixteen officers, only one or two can be spared at one time to go to any type of police training school, thus the officers are never up to date on all the important Supreme Court decisions, since we do not have the funds for in-service training programs.[17]

The above statement was one of the few which indicated a willingness to find ways, especially through training, to work within the newer rules.[18]

The debate in the Senate brought out the question whether the Congress had the power to restrict the appellate jurisdiction of the federal courts. The report to accompany S. 917 included a brief in support of the constitutionality of those sections of the crime bill which would have done that. The brief was prepared at Senator Ervin's request by the American Law Division of the Legislative Reference Service and

16. *Ibid.*, p. 232.
17. *Ibid.*, p. 553.
18. But Superintendent O. W. Wilson of the Chicago Police Department told the senators: "The *Miranda* decision virtually precludes any interrogation by the police. There are those who say that any crime can be solved without interrogation. I would like to state unequivocally that this is simply not so." *Ibid.*, p. 566.

concluded that the restrictions were constitutional.[19] The provision in Article III of the U.S. Constitution reads: "In all Cases affecting Ambassadors, other public Ministers and Consuls, and those in which a State shall be Party, the supreme Court shall have original Jurisdiction. In all the other Cases before mentioned, the supreme Court shall have appellate Jurisdiction, both as to Law and Fact, with such Exceptions, and under such Regulations as the Congress shall make."

The U.S. Supreme Court on several occasions has considered the power of the Congress to regulate its appellate jurisdiction. The first case, apparently, was a 1796 case, *Wiscart* v. *D'Auchy*.[20] The Court held that in the absence of a statute prescribing a rule for appellate proceedings it lacked jurisdiction and if there was one the Court would have to follow it. Fourteen years later Chief Justice Marshall said in the *Durousseau* case[21] that the appellate jurisdiction is derived from the Constitution but any jurisdiction bestowed by Congress with no exceptions implied a denial of all others.

> The appellate powers of this Court are not given by judicial act. They are given by the constitution. But they are limited and regulated by the judicial act, and by such other acts as have been passed on the subject. . . . They have not declared that the appellate power of the court shall not extend to certain cases; but they have described affirmatively its jurisdiction, and this affirmative description has been understood to imply a negative on the exercise of such appellate power as is not comprehended within it.[22]

Some years later, in 1847, the Court decided *Barry* v. *Mercein*.[23] Chief Justice Taney observed that "by the constitution of the United States, the Supreme Court possessed no

19. Report no. 1097 to accompany S. 917, pp. 53–63 (cited above p. 102, n. 15).
20. 3 Dallas 321 (1796). The brief does not list *Wiscart*.
21. 6 Cranch 307 (1810).
22. *Ibid.*, 314.
23. 5 Howard 103.

appellate power in any case, unless conferred upon it by act of Congress, nor can it, when conferred be exercised in any other form, or by any other mode of proceeding than that which the law prescribes."[24]

The subcommittee brief considered the leading case to be *Ex parte McCardle*.[25] It was decided in 1868 and came about from the issues over Reconstruction policies and a controversy between the president and the Congress. In that case the Congress removed jurisdiction of the U.S. Supreme Court even though it had already heard arguments! Even so, Chief Justice Chase dismissed it for want of appellate jurisdiction. He said: "We are not at liberty to inquire into the motives of the legislature. We can only examine into its power under the Constitution; and the power to make exceptions to the appellate jurisdiction of this court is given by express words."[26] As if miffed by the congressional action, he also said, "It is quite clear . . . that this court cannot proceed to pronounce judgment in this case, for it has no longer jurisdiction of the appeal; and judicial duty is not less fitly performed by declining ungranted jurisdiction than in exercising firmly that which the Constitution and the laws confer."[27]

The next year the chief justice said in a case involving the power of the courts in habeas corpus cases that the Congress had given all courts the power to issue the writ and "in law to the Circuit and District Courts is original; that given by the Constitution and the law to this Court is appellate."[28] A few years later Chief Justice Morrison R. Waite said that "it is equally well settled that if a law conferring jurisdiction is repealed without any reservation as to pending cases, all such cases fall with the law."[29]

Supreme Court cases bearing on appellate jurisdiction do not appear to have involved fundamental constitutional

24. *Ibid.*, 119.
25. 6 Wallace 318.
26. *Ibid.*, 514.
27. *Ibid.*, 515.
28. *Ex parte Yerger*, 8 Wallace 85, 101 (1869).
29. *Railroad Company* v. *Grant*, 98 U.S. 398, 401 (1878).

rights of the individual. One clue whether statutory curtailment of appellate jurisdiction would be sustained in such instances is a comment by the first Justice John M. Harlan who in *U.S.* v. *Bitty*, a 1908 case, said that the exception given in the statute in that case "does not violate any constitutional right of the accused." [30]

A more recent case included these words: "It [the Congress] could have declined to create any such courts [appellate courts] leaving suitors to the remedies afforded by state courts, with such appellate review by this Court as Congress might prescribe." [31]

These Supreme Court decisions suggest that the deleted provisions of Title II curbing appellate jurisdiction of the federal courts in state cases might have been a valid exercise of the power of the Congress. But because constitutional rights would have been involved, to have enacted the restrictions could have produced a constitutional crisis between the Court and the Congress. Even with changes in personnel on the appellate courts and the Supreme Court, it is difficult to believe that these courts would have accepted a denial of jurisdiction involving constitutional rights of the individual. In opposing Title II, Senator John C. Pastore (Dem.) of Rhode Island said: "The person title II hurts is that miserable wretch who is apprehended and may not be in a position to know what his constitutional rights are." [32]

Many Senators and members of the House who opposed the provisions of Title II must have thought of Justice Oliver Wendell Holmes, Jr.'s admonition: "I do not think the United States could come to an end if we lost our power to declare an Act of Congress void. I do think the Union would be imperiled if we could not make that declaration as to the laws of the several states." [33] Justice Joseph Story had written in the early case of *Martin* v. *Hunter's Lessee* in 1816, that there was

30. 208 U.S. 393.
31. *Lockerty* v. *Phillips*, 319 U.S. 182, 187 (1943).
32. *Congressional Record*, 90th Cong., 2nd sess., May 21, 1968, 14140.
33. O. W. Holmes, *Collected Legal Papers* (New York: Harcourt, Brace, 1920), pp. 295–96.

the importance, and even necessity of *uniformity* of decisions throughout the whole United States, upon all subjects within the purview of the Constitution. Judges of equal learning and integrity, in different States, might differently interpret a statute, or a treaty of the United States, or even the Constitution itself. If there were no revising authority to control these jarring and discordant judgments, and harmonize them into uniformity, the laws, the treaties, and the Constitution of the United States would be different in different States, and might perhaps never have precisely the same constitution, obligation, or efficacy in any two States. The public mischiefs that would attend such a state of things would be truly deplorable; and it cannot be believed that they could have escaped the enlightened convention which formed the Constitution. What, indeed, might then have been only prophecy has not become fact: and the appellate jurisdiction must continue to be the only adequate remedy for such evils." [34]

As Alexander Hamilton wrote in *The Federalist* No. 78, "The interpretation of the laws is the proper and peculiar province of the courts . . . the Constitution ought to be preferred to the statute, the intention of the people to the intention of their agents." [35]

And in *The Federalist* No. 80, he wrote of the supremacy of the Constitution as the supreme law of the land and a judicial system which prevents a "hydra in government from which nothing but contradiction and confusion can proceed." [36]

34. 1 Wheaton 304, 347, 348.

35. *The Federalist* (Washington, D.C.: National Home Library Edition, 1937), p. 506.

36. *Ibid.*, p. 516.

Mallory v. United States

Justice Frankfurter delivered the opinion of the Court, saying in part:

Petitioner was convicted of rape in the United States District Court for the District of Columbia, and, as authorized by the District Code, the jury imposed a death sentence. The Court of Appeals affirmed, one judge dissenting. . . . Since an important question involving the interpretation of the Federal Rules of Criminal Procedure was involved in this capital case, we granted the petition for certiorari. . . .

The rape occurred at six p.m. on April 7, 1954, in the basement of the apartment house inhabited by the victim. She had descended to the basement a few minutes previous to wash some laundry. Experiencing some difficulty in detaching a hose in the sink, she sought help from the janitor, who lived in a basement apartment with his wife, two grown sons, a younger son and the petitioner, his nineteen-year old half-brother. Petitioner was alone in the apartment at the time. He detached the hose and returned to his quarters. Very shortly thereafter, a masked man, whose general features were identified to resemble those of petitioner and his two grown nephews, attacked the woman. She had heard no one descend the wooden steps that furnished the only means of entering the basement from above.

Petitioner and one of his grown nephews disappeared from the apartment house shortly after the crime was committed.

Reprinted from 354 U.S. 449 (1957).

The former was apprehended the following afternoon between two and two-thirty p.m. and was taken, along with his older nephews, also suspects, to police headquarters. At least four officers questioned him there in the presence of other officers for thirty to forty-five minutes, beginning the examination by telling him, according to his testimony, that his brother had said that he was the assailant. Petitioner strenuously denied his guilt. He spent the rest of the afternoon at headquarters, in the company of the other two suspects and his brother a good part of the time. About four p.m. the three suspects were asked to submit to "lie detector" tests, and they agreed. The officer in charge of the polygraph machine was not located for almost two hours, during which time the suspects received food and drink. The nephews were then examined first. Questioning of petitioner began just after eight p.m. Only he and the polygraph operator were present in a small room, the door to which was closed.

Following almost an hour and one-half of steady interrogation, he "first stated that he could have done this crime, or that he might have done it. He finally stated that he was responsible." . . . Not until ten p.m., after petitioner had repeated his confession to other officers, did the police attempt to reach a United States Commissioner for the purpose of arraignment. Failing in this, they obtained petitioner's consent to examination by the deputy coroner, who noted no indicia of physical or psychological coercion. Petitioner was then confronted by the complaining witness and "practically every man in the Sex Squad," and in response to questioning by three officers, he repeated the confession. Between eleven-thirty p.m. and twelve-thirty a.m. he dictated the confession to a typist. The next morning he was brought before a Commissioner. At the trial, which was delayed for a year because of doubt about petitioner's capacity to understand the proceedings against him, the signed confession was introduced in evidence.

The case calls for the proper application of Rule 5(a) of the Federal Rules of Criminal Procedure, promulgated in 1946 . . . . That Rule provides:

(a) Appearance before the Commissioner.

An officer making an arrest under a warrant issued upon a complaint or any person making an arrest without a warrant shall take the arrested person without unnecessary delay before the nearest available commissioner or before any other nearby officer empowered to commit persons charged with offenses against the laws of the United States. When a person arrested without a warrant is brought before a commissioner or other officer, a complaint shall be filed forthwith.

This provision has both statutory and judicial antecedents for guidance in applying it. The requirement that arraignment be "without unnecessary delay" is a compendious restatement, without substantive change, of several prior specific federal statutory provisions. . . . Nearly all the States have similar enactments.

In *McNabb* v. *United States*, 318 U.S. 332, 343-344, we spelled out the important reasons of policy behind this body of legislation:

The purpose of this impressively pervasive requirement of criminal procedure is plain. . . . The awful instruments of the criminal law cannot be entrusted to a single functionary. The complicated process of criminal justice is therefore divided into different parts, responsibility for which is separately vested in the various participants upon whom the criminal law relied for its vindication. Legislation such as this, requiring that the police must with reasonable promptness show legal cause for detaining arrested persons, constitutes an important safeguard—not only in assuring protection for the innocent but also in securing conviction of the guilty by methods that commend themselves to a progressive and self-confident society. For this procedural requirement checks resort to those reprehensible practices known as the "third degree" which, though universally rejected as indefensible, still find their way into use. It aims to avoid all the evil implications of secret interrogation of persons accused of crime.

Since such unwarranted detention led to tempting utilization of intensive interrogation, easily gliding into the evils of "the third degree," the Court held that police detention of defendants beyond the time when a committing magistrate was readily accessible constituted "willful disobedience of the law." In order adequately to enforce the congressional requirement of prompt arraignment, it was necessary to render inadmissible incriminating statements elicited from defendants during a period of unlawful detention. . . .

The requirement of Rule 5(a) is part of the procedure devised by Congress for safeguarding individual rights without hampering effective and intelligent law enforcement. Provisions related to Rule 5(a) contemplate a procedure that allows arresting officers little more leeway than the interval between arrest and the ordinary administrative steps required to bring a suspect before the nearest available magistrate. . . .

The scheme for initiating a federal prosecution is plainly defined. The police may not arrest upon mere suspicion but only on "probable cause." The next step in the proceeding is to arraign the arrested person before a judicial officer as quickly as possible so that he may be advised of his rights and so that the issue of probable cause may be promptly determined. The arrested person may, of course, be "booked" by the police. But he is not to be taken to police headquarters in order to carry out a process of inquiry that lends itself, even if not so designed, to eliciting damaging statements to support the arrest and ultimately his guilt.

The duty enjoined upon arresting officers to arraign "without unnecessary delay" indicates that the command does not call for mechanical or automatic obedience. Circumstances may justify a brief delay between arrest and arraignment, as for instance, where the story volunteered by the accused is susceptible of quick verification through third parties. But the delay must not be of a nature to give opportunity for the extraction of a confession.

The circumstances of this case preclude a holding that arraignment was "without unnecessary delay." Petitioner was arrested in the early afternoon and was detained at headquarters within the vicinity of numerous committing magistrates. Even though the police had ample evidence from other sources than the petitioner for regarding the petitioner as the chief suspect, they first questioned him for approximately a half hour. When this inquiry of a nineteen-year-old lad of limited intelligence produced no confession, the police asked him to submit to a "lie-detector" test. He was not told of his rights to counsel or to a preliminary examination before a magistrate, nor was he warned that he might keep silent and "that any statement made by him may be used against him." After four hours of further detention at headquarters, during which arraignment could easily have been made in the same building in which police headquarters were housed, petitioner was examined by the lie-detector operator for another hour and a half before his story began to waver. Not until he had confessed, when any judicial caution had lost its purpose, did the police arraign him.

We cannot sanction this extended delay, resulting in confession, without subordinating the general rule of prompt arraignment to the discretion of arresting officers in finding exceptional circumstances for its disregard. In every case where the police resort to interrogation of an arrested person and secure a confession, they may well claim, and quite sincerely, that they were merely trying to check on the information given by him. Against such a claim and the evil potentialities of the practice for which it is urged stands Rule 5(a) as a barrier. Nor is there an escape from the constraint laid upon the police by that Rule in that two other suspects were involved for the same crime. Presumably, whomever the police arrest they must arrest on "probable cause." It is not the function of the police to arrest, as it were, at large and to use an interrogating process at police headquarters in order to determine whom they should charge before a committing magistrate on "probable cause."

Reversed and remanded.

Miranda v. Arizona

Chief Justice Warren delivered the opinion of the Court, saying in part:
  The cases before us raise questions which go to the roots of
our concepts of American criminal jurisprudence: the restraints society must observe consistent with the Federal Constitution in prosecuting individuals for crime. More specifically,
we deal with the admissibility of statements obtained from an
individual who is subjected to custodial police interrogation
and the necessity for procedures which assure that the individual is accorded his privilege under the Fifth Amendment
to the Constitution not to be compelled to incriminate
himself. . . .
  We start here, as we did in *Escobedo*, with the premise that
our holding is not an innovation in our jurisprudence, but is
an application of principles long recognized and applied in
other settings. We have undertaken a thorough re-examination
of the *Escobedo* decision and the principles it announced, and
we reaffirm it. That case was but an explication of basic
rights that are enshrined in our Constitution—that "No
person . . . shall be compelled in any criminal case to be a
witness against himself," and that "the accused shall . . .
have the Assistance of Counsel"—rights which were put in
jeopardy in that case through official overbearing. These
precious rights were fixed in our Constitution only after
centuries of persecution and struggle. And in the words of

Reprinted from 384 U.S. 436 (1966).

Chief Justice Marshall, they were secured "for ages to come and . . . designed to approach immortality as nearly as human institutions can approach it." . . .

Our holding will be spelled out with some specificity in the pages which follow but briefly stated it is this: the prosecution may not use statements, whether exculpatory or inculpatory, stemming from the custodial interrogation of the defendant unless it demonstrates the use of procedural safeguards effective to secure the privilege against self-incrimination. By custodial interrogation, we mean questioning initiated by law enforcement officers after a person has been taken into custody or otherwise deprived of his freedom of action in any significant way. As for the procedural safeguards to be employed, unless other fully effective means are devised to inform accused persons of their right of silence and to assure a continuous opportunity to exercise it, the following measures are required. Prior to any questioning, the person must be warned that he has a right to remain silent, that any statement he does make may be used as evidence against him, and that he has a right to the presence of an attorney, either retained or appointed. The defendant may waive effectuation of these rights, provided the waiver is made voluntarily, knowingly and intelligently. If, however, he indicates in any manner and at any stage of the process that he wishes to consult with an attorney before speaking there can be no questioning. Likewise, if the individual is alone and indicates in any manner that he does not wish to be interrogated, the police may not question him. The mere fact that he may have answered some questions or volunteered some statements on his own does not deprive him of the right to refrain from answering any further inquiries until he has consulted with an attorney and thereafter consents to be questioned.

I

The constitutional issue we decide in each of these cases is the admissibility of statements obtained from a defendant questioned while in custody or otherwise deprived of his freedom of action in any significant way. In each, the defendant was questioned by police officers, detectives, or a prosecuting attorney in a room in which he was cut off from the outside world. In none of these cases was the defendant given a full and effective warning of his rights at the outset of the interrogation process. In all the cases, the questioning elicited oral admissions, and in three of them, signed statements as well which were admitted at their trials. They all thus share salient features—incommunicado interrogation of individuals, in a police-dominated atmosphere, resulting in self-incriminating statements without full warnings of constitutional rights.

An understanding of the nature and setting of this in-custody interrogation is essential to our decisions today. The difficulty in depicting what transpires at such interrogations stems from the fact that in this country they have largely taken place incommunicado. From extensive factual studies undertaken in the early 1930's, including the famous Wickersham Report to Congress by a Presidential Commission, it is clear that police violence and the "third degree" flourished at that time. In a series of cases decided by this Court long after these studies, the police resorted to physical brutality—beatings, hanging, whipping—and to sustained and protracted questioning incommunicado in order to extort confessions. The Commission on Civil Rights in 1961 found much evidence to indicate that "some policemen still resort to physical force to obtain confessions." . . . The use of physical brutality and violence is not, unfortunately, relegated to the past or to any part of the country. Only recently in Kings County, New York, the police brutally beat, kicked and placed lighted cigarette butts on the back of a potential witness under interrogation for the purpose of securing a statement incriminating a third party. . . .

The examples given above are undoubtedly the exception now, but they are sufficiently widespread to be the object of concern. Unless a proper limitation upon custodial interrogation is achieved—such as these decisions will advance—there can be no assurance that practices of this nature will be eradicated in the forseeable future. . . .

Again we stress that the modern practice of in-custody interrogation is psychologically rather than physically oriented. As we have stated before, "Since *Chambers* v. *Florida,* 309 U.S. 227, this Court has recognized that coercion can be mental as well as physical, and that the blood of the accused is not the only hallmark of an unconstitutional inquisition." *Blackburn* v. *Alabama,* 361 U.S. 199, 206 (1960). Interrogation still takes place in privacy. Privacy results in secrecy and this in turn results in a gap in our knowledge as to what in fact goes on in the interrogation rooms. A valuable source of information about present police practices, however, may be found in various police manuals and texts which document procedures employed with success in the past, and which recommend various other effective tactics. These texts are used by law enforcement agencies themselves as guides. It should be noted that these texts professedly present the most enlightened and effective means presently used to obtain statements through custodial interrogation. By considering these texts and other data, it is possible to describe procedures observed and noted around the country.

The officers are told by the manuals that the "principal psychological factor contributing to a successful interrogation is *privacy*—being alone with the person under interrogation. . . .

The texts thus stress that the major qualities an interrogator should possess are patience and perseverance. . . .

The manuals suggest that the suspect be offered legal excuses for his actions in order to obtain an initial admission of guilt. . . .

The interrogators sometimes are instructed to induce a confession out of trickery. The technique here is quite effective in crimes which require identification or which run in series. . . .

The manuals also contain instructions for police on how to handle the individual who refuses to discuss the matter entirely, or who asks for an attorney or relatives. The examiner is to concede to him the right to remain silent. "This usually has a very undermining effect. First of all, he is disappointed in his expectation of an unfavorable reaction on the part of the interrogator. Secondly, a concession of this right to remain silent impresses the subject with the apparent fairness of his interrogator." . . .

From these representative samples of interrogation techniques, the setting prescribed by the manuals and observed in practice becomes clear. In essence, it is this: To be alone with the subject is essential to prevent distraction and to deprive him of any outside support. The aura of confidence in his guilt undermines his will to resist. He merely confirms the preconceived story the police seek to have him describe. Patience and persistence, at times relentless questioning are employed. To obtain a confession, the interrogator must "patiently maneuver himself or his quarry into a position from which the desired objective may be obtained." When normal procedures fail to produce the needed result, the police may resort to deceptive stratagems such as giving false legal advice. It is important to keep the subject off balance, for example, by trading on his insecurity about himself or his surroundings. The police then persuade, trick or cajole him out of exercising his constitutional rights.

Even without employing brutality, the "third degree" or the specific stratagems described above, the very fact of custodial interrogation exacts a heavy toll on individual liberty and trades on the weakness of individuals. This fact may be illustrated simply by referring to three confession cases decided by this Court in the Term immediately preceding our *Escobedo* decision. In *Townsend* v. *Sain*, 372 U.S. 293 (1963), the defendant was a 19-year old heroin addict, described as a "near mental defective." . . . The defendant in *Lynuum* v. *Illinois*, 372 U.S. 528 (1963), was a woman who confessed to the arresting officer after being importuned to "cooperate" in order to prevent her children from being taken by relief authorities. This Court similarly reversed the conviction of a defendant in *Haynes* v. *Washington*, 373 U.S. 503 (1963), whose persistent request during his interrogation was to phone his wife or attorney. In other settings, these individuals might have exercised their constitutional rights. In the incommunicado police-dominated atmosphere, they succumbed.

In the cases before us today, given this background, we

concern ourselves primarily with this interrogation atmosphere and the evils it can bring. In No. 759, *Miranda* v. *Arizona*, the police arrested the defendant and took him to a special interrogation room where they secured a confession. In No. 760, *Vignera* v. *New York*, the defendant made oral admissions to the police after interrogation in the afternoon, and then signed an inculpatory statement upon being questioned by an assistant district attorney later the same evening. In No. 761, *Westover* v. *U.S.*, the defendant was handed over to the Federal Bureau of Investigation by local authorities after they had detained and interrogated him for a lengthy period, both at night and the following morning. After some two hours of questioning, the federal officers had obtained signed statements from the defendant. Lastly, in No. 584, *California* v. *Stewart*, the local police held the defendant five days in the station and interrogated him on nine separate occasions before they secured his inculpatory statement.

In these cases, we might not find the defendant's statements to have been involuntary in traditional terms. Our concern for adequate safeguards to protect precious Fifth Amendment rights is, of course, not lessened in the slightest. In each of the cases, the defendant was thrust into an unfamiliar atmosphere and run through menacing police interrogation procedures. The potentiality for compulsion is forcefully apparent, for example, in *Miranda*, where the indigent Mexican defendant was a seriously disturbed individual with pronounced sexual fantasies, and in *Stewart*, in which the defendant was an indigent Los Angeles Negro who had dropped out of school in the sixth grade. To be sure, the records do not evince overt physical coercion or patented psychological ploys. The fact remains that in none of these cases did the officers undertake to afford appropriate safeguards at the outset of the interrogation to insure that the statements were truly the product of free choice.

It is obvious that such an interrogation environment is created for no purpose other than to subjugate the individual to the will of his examiner. This atmosphere carries its own badge of intimidation. To be sure, this is not physical intimidation, but it is equally destructive of human dignity. The current practice of incommunicado interrogation is at odds with one of our Nation's most cherished principles—that the individual may not be compelled to incriminate himself. Unless adequate protective devices are employed to dispel the compulsion inherent in custodial surroundings, no statement obtained from the defendant can truly be the product of his free choice.

From the foregoing, we can readily perceive an intimate connection between the privilege against self-incrimination and police custodial questioning. . . .

We sometimes forget how long it has taken to establish the privilege against self-incrimination, the sources from which it came and the fervor with which it was defended. Its roots go back into ancient times. . . . Those who framed our Constitution and the Bill of Rights were ever aware of subtle encroachments on individual liberty. They knew that "illegitimate and unconstitutional practices get their first footing . . . by silent approaches and slight deviations from legal modes of procedure." . . . We cannot depart from this noble heritage.

II

. . . As a "noble principle often transcends its origins," the privilege has come rightfully to be recognized in part as an individual's substantive right, a "right to a private enclave where he may lead a private life. That right is the hallmark of our democracy." . . . We have recently noted that the privilege against self-incrimination—the essential mainstay of our adversary system—is founded on a complex of values. . . . All these policies point to one overriding thought: the constitutional foundation underlying the privilege is the respect a government—state or federal—must accord to the dignity and integrity of its citizens. To maintain a "fair state-individual balance," to require the government "to shoulder the entire load," . . . to respect the inviolability of the human personality, our accusatory system of criminal justice demands that the government seeking to punish an individual produce the evidence against him by its own independent labors, rather than by the cruel, simple expedient of compelling it from his own mouth. . . . In sum, the privilege is fulfilled only when the person is guaranteed the right "to remain silent unless he chooses to speak in the unfettered exercise of his own will." . . .

The question in these cases is whether the privilege is fully applicable during a period of custodial interrogation. In this Court, the privilege has consistently been accorded a liberal construction. . . . We are satisfied that all the principles embodied in the privilege apply to informal compulsion exerted by law-enforcement officers during in-custody questioning. An individual swept from familiar surroundings into police custody, surrounded by antagonistic forces, and subjected to the techniques of persuasion described above cannot be otherwise than under compulsion to speak. As a practical matter, the compulsion to speak in the isolated setting of the police station may well be greater than in courts or other official investigations, where there are often impartial observers to guard against intimidation or trickery.

This question, in fact, could have been taken as settled in federal courts almost 70 years ago, when, in *Bram* v. *United States*, 168 U.S. 532, 542 (1897), this Court held:

> In criminal trials, in the courts of the United States, wherever a question arises whether a confession is incompetent because not voluntary, the issue is controlled by that portion of the Fifth Amendment . . . commanding that no person "shall be compelled in any criminal case to be a witness against himself."

. . . Our decision in *Malloy* v. *Hogan*, 378 U.S. 1 (1964), necessitates an examination of the scope of the privilege in state cases as well. In *Malloy*, we squarely held the privilege applicable to the States, and held that the substantive standards underlying the privilege applied with full force to state court proceedings. There, as in *Murphy* v. *Waterfront Comm'n*, 378 U.S. 52 (1964), and *Griffin* v. *California*, 380 U.S. 609 (1965), we applied the existing Fifth Amendment standards to the case before us. Aside from the holding itself, the reasoning in *Malloy* made clear what had already become apparent —that the substantive and procedural safeguards surrounding admissibility of confessions in state cases had become exceedingly exacting, reflecting all the policies embedded in the privilege. The voluntariness doctrine in the state cases, as *Malloy* indicates, encompasses all interrogation practices which are likely to exert such pressure upon an individual as to disable him from making a free and rational choice. The implications of this proposition were elaborated in our decision in *Escobedo* v. *Illinois*, 378 U.S. 478, decided one week after *Malloy* applied the privilege to the States.

Our holding there stressed the fact that the police had not advised the defendant of his constitutional privilege to remain silent at the outset of the interrogation, and we drew attention to that fact at several points in the decision. This was no isolated factor, but an essential ingredient in our decision. The entire thrust of police interrogation there, as in all the cases today, was to put the defendant in such an emotional state as to impair his capacity for rational judgment. The abdication of the constitutional privilege—the choice on his part to speak to the police—was not made knowingly or competently because of the failure to apprise him of his rights; the compelling atmosphere of the in-custody interrogation, and not an independent decision on his part, caused the defendant to speak.

A different phase of the *Escobedo* decision was significant in its attention to the absence of counsel during the questioning. There, as in the cases today, we sought a protective device to dispel the compelling atmosphere of the interrogation. In *Escobedo*, however, the police did not relieve the defendant of the anxieties which they had created in the interrogation rooms. Rather, they denied his request for the assistance of counsel. This heightened his dilemma, and made his later statements the product of this compulsion. The denial of the defendant's request for his attorney thus undermined his ability to exercise the privilege—to remain silent if he chose or to speak without any intimidation, blatant or subtle. The presence of counsel, in all the cases before us today, would be the adequate protective device necessary to make the process of police interrogation conform to the dictates of the privilege. His presence would insure that statements made in the government-established atmosphere are not the product of compulsion.

It was in this manner that *Escobedo* explicated another facet of the pre-trial privilege, noted in many of the Court's prior decisions: the protection of rights at trial. That counsel is present when statements are taken from an individual during interrogation obviously enhances the integrity of the fact-finding processes in court. The presence of an attorney, and the warnings delivered to the individual, enable the defendant under otherwise compelling circumstances to tell his story without fear, effectively, and in a way that eliminates the evils in the interrogation process. . . .

III

Today, then, there can be no doubt that the Fifth Amendment privilege is available outside of criminal court proceedings and serves to protect persons in all settings in which their freedom of action is curtailed from being compelled to incriminate themselves. We have concluded that without proper safeguards the process of in-custody interrogation of persons suspected or accused of crime contains inherently compelling pressures which work to undermine the individual's will to resist and to compel him to speak where he would not otherwise do so freely. In order to combat these pressures and to permit a full opportunity to exercise the privilege against self-incrimination, the accused must be adequately and effectively apprised of his rights and the exercise of those rights must be fully honored.

It is impossible for us to foresee the potential alternatives for protecting the privilege which might be devised by Congress or the States in the exercise of their creative rule-making capacities. Therefore we cannot say that the Constitution necessarily requires adherence to any particular solution for the inherent compulsions of the interrogation process as it is presently conducted. Our decision in no way creates a constitutional straitjacket which will handicap sound efforts at reform, nor is it intended to have this effect. We encourage Congress and the States to continue their laudable search for increasingly efficient enforcement of our criminal laws. However, unless we are showing other procedures which are at least as effective in apprising accused persons of their right of silence and in assuring a continuous opportunity to exercise it, the following safeguards must be observed.

At the outset, if a person in custody is to be subjected to interrogation, he must first be informed in clear and un-equivocal terms that he has the right to remain silent. For those unaware of the privilege, the warning is needed simply to make them aware of it—the threshold requirement for an intelligent decision as to its exercise. More important, such a warning is an absolute prerequisite in overcoming the inherent pressures of the interrogation atmosphere. It is not just the subnormal or woefully ignorant who succumb to an interrogator's imprecations, whether implied or expressly stated, that the interrogation will continue until a confession is obtained or that silence in the face of accusation is itself damning and will abode ill when presented to a jury. Further, the warning will show the individual that his interrogators are prepared to recognize his privilege should he choose to exercise it.

The Fifth Amendment privilege is so fundamental to our system of constitutional rule and the expedient of giving an adequate warning as to the availability of the privilege so simple, we will not pause to inquire in individual cases whether the defendant was aware of his rights without a warning being given. Assessments of the knowledge the defendant possessed, based on information as to his age, education, intelligence, or prior contact with authorities, can never be more than speculation; a warning is a clearcut fact. More important, whatever the background of the person interrogated, a warning at the time of the interrogation is indispensable to overcome its pressures and to insure that the individual knows he is free to exercise the privilege at that point in time.

The warning of the right to remain silent must be accompanied by the explanation that anything said can and will be used against the individual in court. This warning is needed in order to make him aware not only of the privilege, but also of the consequences of foregoing it. It is only through an awareness of these consequences that there can be any assurance of real understanding and intelligent exercise of the privilege. Moreover, this warning may serve to make the individual more acutely aware that he is faced with a phase of the adversary system—that he is not in the presence of persons acting solely in his interest.

The circumstances surrounding in-custody interrogation can operate very quickly to overbear the will of one merely made aware of his privilege by his interrogators. Therefore, the right to have counsel present at the interrogation is indispensable to the protection of the Fifth Amendment privilege under the system we delineate today. Our aim is to assure that the individual's right to choose between silence and speech remains unfettered throughout the interrogation process. A once-stated warning, delivered by those who will conduct the interrogation, cannot itself suffice to that end among those who most require knowledge of their rights. A mere warning given by the interrogators is not alone sufficient to accomplish that end. Prosecutors themselves claim that the admonishment of the right to remain silent without more "will benefit only the recidivist and the professional." . . . Even preliminary advice given to the accused by his own attorney can be swiftly overcome by the secret interrogation process. . . . Thus, the need for counsel to protect the Fifth Amendment privilege comprehends not merely a right to consult with counsel prior to questioning, but also to have counsel present during any questioning if the defendant so desires.

The presence of counsel at the interrogation may serve several significant subsidiary functions as well. If the accused decides to talk to his interrogators, the assistance of counsel can mitigate the dangers of untrustworthiness. With a lawyer present the likelihood that the police will practice coercion is reduced, and if coercion is nevertheless exercised the lawyer can testify to it in court. The presence of a lawyer can also help to guarantee that the accused gives a fully accurate statement to the police and that the statement is rightly reported by the prosecution at trial. . . .

An individual need not make a pre-interrogation request for a lawyer. While such request affirmatively secures his right to have one, his failure to ask for a lawyer does not constitute a waiver. No effective waiver of the right to counsel during interrogation can be recognized unless specifically made after the warnings we here delineate have been given. The accused who does not know his rights and therefore does not make a request may be the person who most needs counsel. . . .

Accordingly we hold that an individual held for interrogation must be clearly informed that he has the right to consult with a lawyer and to have the lawyer with him during interrogation under the system for protecting the privilege we delineate today. As with the warning of the right to remain silent and that anything stated can be used in evidence against him, this warning is an absolute prerequisite to interrogation. No amount of circumstantial evidence that the person may have been aware of this right will suffice to stand in its stead. Only through such a warning is there ascertainable assurance that the accused was aware of this right.

If an individual indicates that he wishes the assistance of counsel before any interrogation occurs, the authorities cannot rationally ignore or deny his request on the basis that the individual does not have or cannot afford a retained attorney. The financial ability of the individual has no relationship to the scope of the rights involved here. The privilege against self-incrimination secured by the Constitution applies to all individuals. The need for counsel in order to protect the privilege exists for the indigent as well as the affluent. In fact, were we to limit these constitutional rights to those who can retain an attorney, our decisions today would be of little significance. These cases before us as well as the vast majority of confession cases with which we have dealt in the past involve those unable to retain counsel. While authorities are not required to relieve the accused of his poverty, they have the obligation not to take advantage of indigence in the administration of justice. Denial of counsel to the indigent at the time of interrogation while allowing an attorney to those who can afford one would be no more supportable by reason or logic than the similar situation at trial and on appeal struck down in *Gideon* v. *Wainwright,* 372 U.S. 335 (1963), and *Douglas* v. *California,* 372 U.S. 353 (1963).

In order fully to apprise a person interrogated of the extent of his rights under this system then, it is necessary to warn him not only that he has the right to consult with an attorney, but also that if he is indigent a lawyer will be appointed to represent him. Without this additional warning, the admonition of the right to consult with counsel would often be understood as meaning only that he can consult with a lawyer if he has one or has the funds to obtain one. The warning of a right to counsel would be hollow if not couched in terms that would convey to the indigent—the person most often subjected to interrogation—the knowledge that he too has a right to have counsel present. As with the warnings of the right to remain silent and of the general right to counsel, only by effective and express explanation to the indigent of this right can there be assurance that he was truly in a position to exercise it.

Once warnings have been given, the subsequent procedure is clear. If the individual indicates in any manner, at any time prior to or during questioning, that he wishes to remain silent, the interrogation must cease. At this point he has shown that he intends to exercise his Fifth Amendment privilege; any statement taken after the person invokes his privilege cannot be other than the product of compulsion, subtle or otherwise. Without the right to cut off questioning, the setting of in-custody interrogation operates on the individual to overcome free choice in producing a statement after the privilege has been once invoked. If the individual states that he wants an attorney, the interrogation must cease until an attorney is present. At that time, the individual must have an opportunity to confer with the attorney and to have him present during any subsequent questioning. If the individual cannot obtain an attorney and he indicates that he wants one before speaking to police, they must respect his decision to remain silent.

This does not mean, as some have suggested, that each police station must have a "station house lawyer" present at all times to advise prisoners. It does mean, however, that if police propose to interrogate a person they must make known to him that he is entitled to a lawyer and that if he cannot afford one, a lawyer will be provided for him prior to any interrogation. If authorities conclude that they will not provide counsel during a reasonable period of time in which investigation in the field is carried out, they may refrain from doing so without violating the person's Fifth Amendment privilege so long as they do not question him during that time.

If the interrogation continues without the presence of an attorney and a statement is taken, a heavy burden rests on the government to demonstrate that the defendant knowingly and intelligently waived his privilege against self-incrimination and his right to retained or appointed counsel. . . . This Court has always set high standards of proof for the waiver of constitutional rights, *Johnson* v. *Zerbst*, 304 U.S. 458 (1938), and we reassert these standards as applied to in-custody interrogation. Since the State is responsible for establishing the isolated circumstances under which the interrogation takes place and has the only means of making available corroborated evidence of warnings given during incommunicado interrogation, the burden is rightly on its shoulders.

An express statement that the individual is willing to make a statement and does not want an attorney followed closely by a statement could constitute a waiver. But a valid waiver will not be presumed simply from the silence of the accused after warnings are given or simply from the fact that a confession was in fact eventually obtained. . . .

Whatever the testimony of the authorities as to waiver of rights by an accused, the fact of lengthy interrogation or incommunicado incarceration before a statement is made is strong evidence that the accused did not validly waive his rights. In these circumstances the fact that the individual eventually made a statement is consistent with the conclusion that the compelling influence of the interrogation finally forced him to do so. It is inconsistent with any notion of a voluntary relinquishment of the privilege. Moreover, any evidence that the accused was threatened, tricked, or cajoled into a waiver will, of course, show that the defendant did not voluntarily waive his privilege. The requirement of warnings and waiver of rights is a fundamental with respect to the Fifth Amendment privilege and not simply a preliminary ritual to existing methods of interrogation.

The warnings required and the waiver necessary in accordance with our opinion today are, in the absence of a fully effective equivalent, prerequisites to the admissibility of any statement made by a defendant. No distinction can be drawn between statements which are direct confessions and statements which amount to "admissions" of part or all of an offense. The privilege against self-incrimination protects the individual from being compelled to incriminate himself in any manner; it does not distinguish degrees of incrimination. Similarly, for precisely the same reason, no distinction may be drawn between inculpatory statements and statements alleged to be merely "exculpatory." If a statement made were in fact truly exculpatory it would, of course, never be used by the prosecution. In fact, statements merely intended to be exculpatory by the defendants are often used to impeach his testimony at trial or to demonstrate untruths in the statement given under interrogation and thus to prove guilt by implication. These statements are incriminating in any meaningful sense of the word and may not be used without the full warnings and effective waiver required for any other statement. In *Escobedo* itself, the defendant fully intended his accusation of another as the slayer to be exculpatory as to himself.

The principles announced today deal with the protection which must be given to the privilege against self-incrimination when the individual is first subjected to police interrogation while in custody at the station or otherwise deprived of his freedom of action in any significant way. It is at this point that our adversary system of criminal proceedings commences, distinguishing itself at the outset from the inquisitorial system recognized in some countries. Under the system of warnings we delineate today or under any other system which may be devised and found effective, the safeguards to be erected about the privilege must come into play at this point.

Our decision is not intended to hamper the traditional function of police officers in investigating crime. . . . When an individual is in custody on probable cause, the police may, of course, seek out evidence in the field to be used at trial against him. Such investigation may include inquiry of persons not under restraint. General on-the-scene questioning as to facts surrounding a crime or other general questioning of citizens in the fact-finding process is not affected by our holding. It is an act of responsible citizenship for individuals to give volunteer information they may have to aid in law enforcement. In such situations the compelling atmosphere inherent in the process of in-custody interrogation is not necessarily present.

In dealing with statements obtained through interrogation, we do not purport to find all confessions inadmissible. Confessions remain a proper element in law enforcement. Any statement given freely and voluntarily without any compelling influences is, of course, admissible in evidence. The fundamental import of the privilege while an individual is in custody is not whether he is allowed to talk to the police without the benefit of warnings and counsel, but whether he can be interrogated. There is no requirement that police stop a person who enters a police station and states that he wishes to confess to a crime, or a person who calls the police to offer a confession or any other statement he desires to make. Volunteered statements of any kind are not barred by the Fifth Amendment and their admissibility is not affected by our holding today.

To summarize, we hold that when an individual is taken into custody or otherwise deprived of his freedom by the authorities in any significant way and is subjected to questioning, the privilege against self-incrimination is jeopardized. Procedural safeguards must be employed to protect the privilege, and unless other fully effective means are adopted to notify the person of his right of silence and to assure that the exercise of the right will be scrupulously honored, the following measures are required. He must be warned prior to any questioning that he has the right to remain silent, that anything he says can be used against him in a court of law, that he has the right to the presence of an attorney, and that if he cannot afford an attorney one will be appointed for him prior to any questioning if he so desires. Opportunity to exercise the rights must be afforded to him throughout the interrogation. After such warnings have been given, and such opportunity afforded him, the individual may knowingly and intelligently waive these rights and agree to answer questions or make a statement. But unless and until such warnings and waiver are demonstrated by the prosecution at trial, no evidence obtained as a result of interrogation can be used against him.

IV

A recurrent argument made in these cases is that society's need for interrogation outweighs the privilege. This argument is not unfamiliar to this Court. . . . The whole thrust of our foregoing discussion demonstrates that the Constitution has prescribed the rights of the individual when confronted with the power of government when it provided in the Fifth Amendment that an individual cannot be compelled to be a witness against himself. That right cannot be abridged. As Mr. Justice Brandeis once observed:

> Decency, security and liberty alike demand that government officials shall be subjected to the same rules of conduct that are commands to the citizen. In a government of laws, existence of the government will be imperilled if it fails to observe the law scrupulously. Our Government is the potent, the omnipresent teacher. For good or ill, it teaches the whole people by its example. Crime is contagious. If the Government becomes a lawbreaker, it breeds contempt for law; it invites every man to become a law unto himself; it invites anarchy. To declare that in

the administration of the criminal law the end justifies the means . . . would bring terrible retribution. Against that pernicious doctrine this Court should resolutely set its face.

If the individual desires to exercise his privilege, he has the right to do so. This is not for the authorities to decide. An attorney may advise his client not to talk to police until he has had an opportunity to investigate the case, or he may wish to be present with his client during any police questioning. In doing so an attorney is merely exercising the good professional judgment he has been taught. This is not cause for considering the attorney a menace to law enforcement. He is merely carrying out what he is sworn to do under his oath— to protect to the extent of his ability the rights of his client. In fulfilling this responsibility the attorney plays a vital role in the administration of criminal justice under our Constitution.

In announcing these principles, we are not unmindful of the burdens which law enforcement officials must bear, often under trying circumstances. We also fully recognize the obligation of all citizens to aid in enforcing the criminal laws. This Court, while protecting individual rights, has always given ample latitude to law enforcement agencies in the legitimate exercise of their duties. The limits we have placed on the interrogation process should not constitute an undue interference with a proper system of law enforcement. As we have noted, our decision does not in any way preclude police from carrying out their traditional investigatory functions. Although confessions may play an important role in some convictions, the cases before us present graphic examples of the overstatement of the "need" for confessions. In each case authorities conducted interrogations ranging up to five days in duration despite the presence, through standard investigating practices, of considerable evidence against each defendant. . . .

It is also urged that an unfettered right to detention for interrogation should be allowed because it will often redound to the benefit of the person questioned. When police inquiry determines that there is no reason to believe that the person has committed any crime, it is said, he will be released without need for further formal procedures. The person who has committed no offense, however, will be better able to clear himself after warnings, with counsel present than without. It can be assumed that in such circumstances a lawyer would advise his client to talk freely to police in order to clear himself.

Custodial interrogation, by contrast, does not necessarily afford the innocent an opportunity to clear themselves. A serious consequence of the present practice of the interrogation alleged to be beneficial for the innocent is that many arrests "for investigation" subject large numbers of innocent persons to detention and interrogation. . . .

Over the years the Federal Bureau of Investigation has compiled an exemplary record of effective law enforcement while advising any suspect or arrested person, at the outset of an interview, that he is not required to make a statement, that any statement may be used against him in court, that the individual may obtain the services of an attorney of his own choice and, more recently, that he has a right to free counsel if he is unable to pay. A letter received from the Solicitor General in response to a question from the Bench makes it clear that the present pattern of warnings and respect for the rights of the individual followed as a practice by the FBI is consistent with the procedure which we delineate today. . . .

It is also urged upon us that we withhold decision on this issue until state legislative bodies and advisory groups have had an opportunity to deal with these problems by rule making. We have already pointed out that the Constitution does not require any specific code of procedures for protecting the privilege against self-incrimination during custodial interrogation. Congress and the States are free to develop their own safeguards for the privilege, so long as they are fully as effective as those described above in informing accused persons of their right of silence and in affording a continuous opportunity to exercise it. In any event, however, the issues presented are of constitutional dimensions and must be determined by the courts. The admissibility of a statement in the face of a claim that it was obtained in violation of the defendant's constitutional rights is an issue the resolution of which has long since been undertaken by this Court. . . . Judicial solutions to problems of constitutional dimension have evolved decade by decade. As courts have been presented with the need to enforce constitutional rights, they have found means of doing so. . . . Where rights secured by the Constitution are involved, there can be no rule making or legislation which would abrogate them.

V

Because of the nature of the problem and because of its recurrent significance in numerous cases, we have to this point discussed the relationship of the Fifth Amendment privilege to police interrogation without specific concentration on the facts of the cases before us. We now turn to these facts to consider the application to these cases of the constitutional principles discussed above. In each instance, we have concluded that statements were obtained from the defendant under circumstances that did not meet constitutional standards for protection of the privilege.

No. 759. *Miranda* v. *Arizona.*

On March 13, 1963, Petitioner, Ernesto Miranda, was arrested at his home and taken in custody to a Phoenix police station. He was there identified by the complaining witness. The police then took him to "Interrogation Room No. 2" of the detective bureau. There he was questioned by two police officers. The officers admitted at trial that Miranda was not advised that he had a right to have an attorney present. Two hours later, the officers emerged from the interrogation room with a written confession signed by Miranda. At the top of the statement was a typed paragraph stating that the confession was made voluntarily, without threats or promises of immunity and "with full knowledge of my legal rights, understanding any statement I make may be used against me."

At his trial before a jury, the written confession was admitted into evidence over the objection of defense counsel, and the officers testified to the prior oral confession made by Miranda during interrogation. Miranda was found guilty of kidnapping and rape. He was sentenced to 20 to 30 years' imprisonment on each count, the sentences to run concurrently. On appeal, the Supreme Court of Arizona held that Miranda's constitutional rights were not violated in obtaining the confession and affirmed the conviction. . . . In reaching its decision, the court emphasized heavily the fact that Miranda did not specifically request counsel.

We reverse. From the testimony of the officers and by the admission of respondent, it is clear that Miranda was not in any way apprised of his right to consult with an attorney and to have one present during the interrogation, nor was his right not to be compelled to incriminate himself effectively protected in any other manner. Without these warnings the statements were inadmissible. The mere fact that he had signed a statement which contained a typed-in clause stating that he had "full knowledge" of his "legal rights" does not approach the knowing and intelligent waiver required to relinquish constitutional rights. . . .

Justice Clark, dissenting in Nos. 759, 760, and 761 . . .:
The *ipse dixit* of the majority has no support in our cases. Indeed, the Court admits that "we might not find the defendants' statements here to have been involuntary in traditional terms." . . . In short, the Court has added more to the requirements that the accused is entitled to consult with his lawyer and that he must be given the traditional warning that he may remain silent and that anything that he says may be used against him. . . . Now, the Court fashions a constitutional rule that the police may engage in no custodial interrogation without additionally advising the accused that he has a right under the Fifth Amendment to the presence of counsel during interrogation and that, if he is without funds, that counsel will be furnished him. When at any point during an interrogation the accused seeks affirmatively or impliedly to invoke his rights to silence or counsel, interrogation must be forgone or postponed. The Court further holds that failure to follow the

new procedures requires inexorably the exclusion of any statement by the accused, as well as the fruits thereof. Such a strict constitutional specific inserted at the nerve center of crime detection may well kill the patient. Since there is at this time a paucity of information and an almost total lack of empirical knowledge on the practical operation of requirements, truly comparable to those announced by the majority, I would be more restrained lest we go too far too fast. . . . The rule prior to today . . . depended upon "a totality of circumstances evidencing an involuntary . . . admission of guilt. . . .

I would continue to follow that rule. . . . I would consider in each case whether the police officer prior to custodial interrogation added the warning that the suspect might have counsel present at the interrogation and, further, that a court would appoint one at his request if he was too poor to employ counsel. In the absence of warnings, the burden would be on the State to prove that counsel was knowingly and intelligently waived or that the totality of the circumstances, including the failure to give the necessary warnings, the confession was clearly voluntary. . . .

Justice Harlan, whom Justice Stewart and Justice White joined, dissented, in part, saying:

I believe the decision of the Court represents poor constitutional law and entails harmful consequences for the country at large. How serious these consequences may prove to be only time can tell. But the basic flaws in the Court's justification seem to me readily apparent now once all sides of the problem are considered. . . .

While the fine points of this scheme are far less clear than the Court admits, the tenor is quite apparent. The new rules are not designed to guard against police brutality or other unmistakably banned forms of coercion. Those who use third-degree tactics and deny them in court are equally able and destined to lie as skillfully about warnings and waivers. Rather, the thrust of the new rules is to negate all pressures, to reinforce the nervous or ignorant suspect, and ultimately to discourage any confession at all. The aim in short is toward "voluntariness" in a utopian sense, or to view it from a different angle, voluntariness with a vengeance.

To incorporate this notion into the Constitution requires a strained reading of history and precedent and a disregard of the very pragmatic concerns that alone may on occasion justify such strains. . . .

What the Court largely ignores is that its rules impair, if they will not eventually serve wholly to frustrate, an instrument of law enforcement that has long and quite reasonably been thought worth the price paid for it. There can be little doubt that the Court's new code would markedly decrease the number of confessions. To warn the suspect that he may remain silent and remind him that his confession may be used in court are minor obstructions. To require also an express waiver by the suspect and an end to questioning whenever he demurs must heavily handicap questioning. And to suggest or provide counsel for the suspect simply invites the end of the interrogation.

How much harm this decision will inflict on law enforcement cannot fairly be predicted with accuracy. Evidence on the role of confessions is notoriously incomplete, . . . and little is added by the Court's reference to the FBI experience and the resources believed wasted in interrogation. . . . We do know that some crimes cannot be solved without confessions, that ample expert testimony attests to their importance in crime control, and that the Court is taking a real risk with society's welfare in imposing its new regime on the country. The social costs of crime are too great to call the new rules anything but a hazardous experimentation.

While passing over the costs and risks of its experiment, the Court portrays the evils of normal police questioning in terms which I think are exaggerated. Albeit stringently confined by the due process standards interrogation is no doubt often inconvenient and unpleasant for the suspect. However, it is no less so for a man to be arrested and jailed, to have his house searched, or to stand trial in court, yet all this may properly happen to the most innocent given probable cause, a warrant, or an indictment. Society has always paid a stiff price for law

and order, and peaceful interrogation is not one of the dark
moments of the law. . . .

Miranda's oral and written confessions are now held inadmissible under the Court's new rules. One is entitled to feel
astonished that the Constitution can be read to produce this
result. These confessions were obtained during brief, daytime
questioning conducted by two officers and unmarked by any
of the traditional indicia of coercion. . . .

*Justice White, with whom Justice Harlan and Justice Stewart
joined, dissented, in part:*

The proposition that the privilege against self-incrimination
forbids in-custody interrogation without the warning specified
in the majority opinion and without a clear waiver of counsel
has no significant support in the history of the privilege or in
the language of the Fifth Amendment. . . .

Decisions like these cannot rest alone on syllogism, meta-
physics or some ill-defined notions of natural justice, although
each will perhaps play its part. In proceeding to such construction as it now announces, the Court should also duly
consider all the factors and interests bearing upon the cases, at
least insofar as the relevant materials are available; and if the
necessary considerations are not treated in the record or
obtainable from some other reliable source, the Court should
not proceed to formulate fundamental policies based on
speculation alone. . . .

The obvious underpinning of the Court's decision is a deep-
seated distrust of all confessions. As the Court declares that the
accused may not be interrogated without counsel present,
absent a waiver of the right to counsel, and as the Court all
but admonishes the lawyer to advise the accused to remain
silent, the result adds up to a judicial judgment that evidence
from the accused should not be used against him in any way,
whether compelled or not. This is the not so subtle overtone of
the opinion—that it is inherently wrong for the police to
gather evidence from the accused himself. And this is precisely
the nub of this dissent. I see nothing wrong or immoral and
certainly nothing unconstitutional, with the police asking a

suspect whom they have reasonable cause to arrest whether or not he killed his wife or with confronting him with the evidence on which the arrest was based, at least where he has been plainly advised that he may remain completely silent . . . . Moreover, it is by no means certain that the process of confessing is injurious to the accused. To the contrary it may provide psychological relief and enhance the prospects for rehabilitation. . . .

The most basic function of any government is to provide for the security of the individual and of his property. . . . These ends of society are served by the criminal laws which for the most part are aimed at the prevention of crime. Without the reasonably effective performance of the task of preventing private violence and retaliation, it is idle to talk about human dignity and civilized values. . . .

The rule announced today will measurably weaken the ability of the criminal law to perform in these tasks. It is a deliberate calculus to prevent interrogation, to reduce the incidence of confessions and pleas of guilty and to increase the number of trials. . . .

There is, in my view, every reason to believe that a good many criminal defendants, who otherwise would have been convicted on what this Court has previously thought to be the most satisfactory kind of evidence, will now, under this new version of the Fifth Amendment, either not be tried at all or acquitted if the State's evidence, minus the confession, is put to the test of litigation. . . .

United States v. Wade

Justice Brennan delivered the opinion of the Court, saying in part:

The question here is whether courtroom identifications of an accused at trial are to be excluded from evidence because the accused was exhibited to the witnesses before trial at a post-indictment lineup conducted for identification purposes without notice to and in the absence of the accused's appointed counsel.

The federally insured bank in Eustace, Texas, was robbed on September 21, 1964. A man with a small strip of tape on each side of his face entered the bank, pointed a pistol at the female cashier and the vice president, the only persons in the bank at the time, and forced them to fill a pillowcase with the bank's money. The man then drove away with an accomplice who had been waiting in a stolen car outside the bank. On March 23, 1965, an indictment was returned against respondent, Wade, and two others for conspiring to rob the bank, and against Wade and the accomplice for the robbery itself. Wade was arrested on April 2, and counsel was appointed to represent him on April 26. Fifteen days later an FBI agent, without notice to Wade's lawyer, arranged to have the two bank employees observe a lineup made up of Wade and five or six other prisoners and conducted in a courtroom of the local county courthouse. Each person in the line wore strips of tape such as allegedly worn by the robber and upon direction each

Reprinted from 388 U.S. 218 (1967).

said something like "put the money in the bag," the words allegedly uttered by the robber. Both bank employees identified Wade in the lineup as the bank robber.

At trial, the two employees, when asked on direct examination if the robber was in the courtroom, pointed to Wade. The prior lineup identification was then elicited from both employees on cross-examination. At the close of testimony, Wade's counsel moved for a judgment of acquittal or, alternatively, to strike the bank officials' courtroom identifications on the ground that conduct of the lineup, without notice to and in the absence of his appointed counsel, violated his Fifth Amendment privilege against self-incrimination and his Sixth Amendment right to the assistance of counsel. The motion was denied, and Wade was convicted. The Court of Appeals for the Fifth Circuit reversed the conviction and ordered a new trial at which the in-court identification evidence was to be excluded, holding that, though the lineup did not violate Wade's Fifth Amendment rights, "the lineup, held as it was, in the absence of counsel, already chosen to represent appellant, was a violation of his Sixth Amendment rights." . . . We reverse the judgment of the Court of Appeals and remand to that court with direction to enter a new judgment vacating the conviction and remanding the case to the District Court for further proceedings consistent with this opinion.

I

Neither the lineup itself nor anything shown by this record that Wade was required to do in the lineup violated his privilege against self-incrimination. We have only recently reaffirmed that the privilege "protects an accused only from being compelled to testify against himself, or otherwise provide the State with evidence of a testimonial or communicative nature . . . ." We there held that compelling a suspect to submit to a withdrawal of a sample of his blood for analysis for alcohol content and the admission in evidence of the analysis report were not compulsion to those ends. That holding was supported by the opinion in *Holt* v. *United States*, 218 U.S. 245, in which case a question arose as to whether a blouse belonged to the defendant. A witness testified at trial that the defendant put on the blouse and it had fitted him. The defendant argued that the admission of the testimony was error because compelling him to put on the blouse was a violation of his privilege. The Court rejected the claim as "an extravagant extension of the Fifth Amendment," Mr. Justice Holmes saying for the Court:

> The prohibition of compelling a man in a criminal court to be witness against himself is a prohibition of the use of physical or moral compulsion to extort communications from him, not an exclusion of his body as evidence when it may be material.

The Court in *Holt*, however, put aside any constitutional questions which might be involved in compelling an accused, as here, to exhibit himself before victims of or witnesses to an alleged crime; the Court stated, "we need not consider how far a court would go in compelling a man to exhibit himself."

We have no doubt that compelling the accused merely to exhibit his person for observation by a prosecution witness prior to trial involves no compulsion of the accused to give evidence having testimonial significance. It is compulsion of the accused to exhibit his physical characteristics, not compulsion to disclose any knowledge he might have. It is no different from compelling Schmerber to provide a blood sample or Holt to wear the blouse, and, as in those instances, is not within the cover of the privilege. Similarly, compelling Wade to speak within hearing distance of the witnesses, even to utter words purportedly uttered by the robber, was not compulsion to utter statements of a "testimonial" nature; he was required to use his voice as an identifying physical characteristic, not to speak his guilt. We held in *Schmerber* . . ., that the distinction to be drawn under the Fifth Amendment privilege against self-incrimination is one between an accused's "communications" in whatever form, vocal or physical, and "compulsion which makes a suspect or accused the source of 'real or physical evidence,'" . . . . We recognized that "both federal and state courts have usually held that . . . [the privilege] offers no protection against compulsion to submit to fingerprinting, photography, or measurements, to write or speak for identification, to appear in court, to stand, to assume a stance, to walk, or to make a particular gesture." None of these activities becomes testimonial within the scope of the privilege because required of the accused in a pretrial lineup.

Moreover, it deserves emphasis that this case presents no question of the admissibility in evidence of anything Wade said or did at the lineup which implicates his privilege. The Government offered no such evidence as part of its case, and what came out about the lineup proceedings on Wade's cross-examination of the bank employees involved no violation of Wade's privilege.

II

The fact that the lineup involved no violation of Wade's privilege against self-incrimination does not, however, dispose of his contention that the courtroom identifications should have been excluded because the lineup was conducted without notice to and in the absence of his counsel. Our rejection of the right to counsel claim in *Schmerber* rested on our conclusion in that case that "no issue of counsel's ability to assist petitioner in respect of any rights he did possess is presented." In contrast, in this case it is urged that the assistance of counsel at the lineup was indispensable to protect Wade's most basic right as a criminal defendant—his right to a fair trial at which the witnesses against him might be meaningfully cross-examined.

The Framers of the Bill of Rights envisaged a broader role for counsel than under the practice then prevailing in England of merely advising his client in "matters of law," and eschewing any responsibility for "matters of fact." The constitutions in at least 11 of the 13 States expressly or impliedly abolished this distinction. ... When the Bill of Rights was adopted, there were no organized police forces as we know them today. The accused confronted the prosecutor and the witnesses against him, and the evidence was marshalled, largely at the trial itself. In contrast, today's law enforcement machinery involves critical confrontations of the accused by the prosecution at pretrial proceedings where the results might well settle the accused's fate and reduce the trial itself to a mere formality. In recognition of these realities of modern criminal prosecution, our cases have construed the Sixth Amendment guarantee to apply to "critical" stages of the proceedings. The guarantee reads: "In all criminal prosecutions, the accused shall enjoy the right . . . to have the Assistance of Counsel *for his defence*." . . . The plain wording of this guarantee thus encompasses counsel's assistance whenever necessary to assure a meaningful "defence."

. . . It is central to that principle that in addition to counsel's presence at trial, the accused is guaranteed that he need not stand alone against the State at any stage of the prosecution, formal or informal, in court or out, where counsel's absence might derogate from the accused's rights to a fair trial. The security of that right is as much the aim of the right to counsel as it is of the other guarantees of the Sixth Amendment—the right of the accused to a speedy and public trial by an impartial jury, his right to be informed of the nature and cause of the accusation, and his right to be confronted with the witnesses against him and to have compulsory process for obtaining witnesses in his favor. The presence of counsel at such critical confrontations, as at the trial itself, operates to assure that the accused's interests will be protected consistently with our adversary theory of criminal prosecution.

In sum . . . it is necessary to preserve the defendant's basic right to a fair trial as affected by his right meaningfully to cross-examine the witnesses against him and to have effective assistance of counsel at the trial itself. It calls upon us to analyze whether potential substantial prejudice to defendant's rights inheres in the particular confrontation and the ability of counsel to help avoid that prejudice.

III

The Government characterizes the lineup as a mere preparatory step in the gathering of the prosecution's evidence, not different—for Sixth Amendment purposes—from various other preparatory steps, such as systematized or scientific analyzing of the accused's fingerprints, blood sample, clothing, hair, and the like. We think there are differences which preclude such stages being characterized as critical stages at which the accused has the right to the presence of his counsel. Knowledge of the techniques of science and technology is sufficiently available, and the variables in techniques few enough, that the accused has the opportunity for a meaningful confrontation of the Government's case at trial through the ordinary processes of cross-examination of the Government's expert witnesses and the presentation of the evidence of his own experts. The denial of a right to have his counsel present at such analyses does not therefore violate the Sixth Amendment; they are not critical stages since there is minimal risk that his counsel's absence at such stages might derogate from his right to a fair trial.

IV

But the confrontation compelled by the State between the accused and the victim or witnesses to a crime to elicit identification evidence is peculiarly riddled with innumerable dangers and variable factors which might seriously, even crucially, derogate from a fair trial. The vagaries of eyewitness identification are well-known; the annals of criminal law are rife with instances of mistaken identification. . . . A major factor contributing to the high incidence of miscarriage of justice from mistaken identification has been the degree of suggestion inherent in the manner in which the prosecution presents the suspect to witnesses for pretrial identification. A commentator has observed that "the influence of improper suggestion upon identifying witnesses probably accounts for more miscarriages of justice than any other single factor—perhaps it is responsible for more such errors than all other factors combined." . . . Suggestion can be created intentionally or unintentionally in many subtle ways. And the dangers for the suspect are particularly grave when the witness' opportunity for observation was substantial, and thus his susceptibility to suggestion the greatest.

Moreover, "it is a matter of common experience that, once a witness has picked out the accused at the line-up, he is not likely to go back on his word later on, so that in practice the issue of identity may (in the absence of other relevant evidence) for all practical purposes be determined there and then, before the trial."

. . . It is obvious that risks of suggestion attend either form of confrontation and increase the dangers inhering in eye-witness identification. But as is the case with secret interrogations, there is serious difficulty in depicting what transpires at lineups and other forms of identification confrontations. "Privacy results in secrecy and this in turn results in a gap in our knowledge as to what in fact goes on. . . ." For the same reasons, the defense can seldom reconstruct the manner and mode of lineup identification for judge or jury at trial. Those participating in a lineup with the accused may often be police officers; in any event, the participants' names are rarely recorded or divulged at trial. The impediments to an objective observation are increased when the victim is the witness. Lineups are prevalent in rape and robbery prosecutions and present a particular hazard that a victim's participants are apt to be alert for conditions prejudicial to the suspect. And if they were, it would likely be of scant benefit to the suspect since neither witnesses nor lineup participants are likely to be schooled in the detection of suggestive influences. Improper influences may go undetected by a suspect, guilty or not, who experiences the emotional tension which we might expect in one being confronted with potential accusers. Even when he does observe abuse, if he has a criminal record he may be reluctant to take the stand and open up the admission of prior convictions. Moreover, any protestations by the suspect of the fairness of the lineup made at trial are likely to be in vain; the jury's choice is between the accused's unsupported version and that of the police officers present. In short, the accused's inability effectively to reconstruct at trial any unfairness that occurred at the lineup may deprive him of his only opportunity meaningfully to attack the credibility of the witness' courtroom identification. . . .

The potential for improper influence is illustrated by the circumstances, insofar as they appear, surrounding the prior identifications in the three cases we decide today. In the present case, the testimony of the identifying witnesses elicited on cross-examination revealed that those witnesses were taken to the courthouse and seated in the courtroom to await assembly of the lineup. The courtroom faced on a hallway observable to the witnesses through an open door. The cashier testified that she saw Wade "standing in the hall" within sight of an FBI agent. Five or six other prisoners later appeared in the hall. The vice president testified that he saw a person in the hall in the custody of the agent who "resembled the person that we identified as the one who had entered the bank."

. . . It is hard to imagine a situation more clearly conveying the suggestion to the witness that the one presented is believed guilty by the police.

The few cases that have surfaced therefore reveal the existence of a process attended with hazards of serious unfairness to the criminal accused and strongly suggest the plight of the more numerous defendants who are unable to ferret out suggestive influences in the secrecy of the confrontation. We do not assume that these risks are the result of police procedures intentionally designed to prejudice an accused. Rather we assume they derive from the dangers inherent in eyewitness identification and the suggestibility inherent in the context of the pretrial identification. . . .

Insofar as the accused's conviction may rest on a courtroom identification in fact the fruit of a suspect pretrial identification which the accused is helpless to subject to effective scrutiny at trial, the accused is deprived of that right of cross-examination which is an essential safeguard to his right to confront the witnesses against him. And even though cross-examination is a precious safeguard to a fair trial, it cannot be viewed as an absolute assurance of accuracy and reliability. . . . The trial which might determine the accused's fate may well not be that in the courtroom but that at the pretrial confrontation, with the State aligned against the accused, the witness the sole jury, and the accused unprotected against the overreaching, intentional or unintentional, and with little or no effective appeal from the judgment there rendered by the witness—"that's the man."

Since it appears that there is grave potential for prejudice, intentional or not, in the pretrial lineup, which may not be capable of reconstruction at trial, and since presence of counsel itself can often avert prejudice and assure a meaningful confrontation at trial, there can be little doubt that for Wade the post-indictment lineup was a critical stage of the prosecution at which he was "as much entitled to such aid [of counsel] . . . as at the trial itself." Thus both Wade and his counsel should have been notified of the impending lineup, and counsel's presence should have been a requisite to conduct of the lineup, absent an "intelligent waiver." No substantial counterprevailing policy considerations have been advanced against the requirement of the presence of counsel. Concern is expressed that the requirement will forestall prompt identifications and result in obstruction of the confrontations. As for the first, we note that in the two cases in which the right to counsel is today held to apply, counsel had already been appointed and no argument is made in either case that notice to counsel would have prejudicially delayed the confrontations. Moreover, we leave open the question whether the presence of substitute counsel might not suffice where notification and presence of the suspect's own counsel would result in prejudicial delay. And to refuse to recognize the right to counsel for fear that counsel will obstruct the course of justice is contrary to the basic assumptions upon which this Court has operated in Sixth Amendment cases. . . . In our view counsel can hardly impede legitimate law enforcement; on the contrary, for the reasons expressed, law enforcement may be assisted by preventing the infiltration of taint in the prosecution's identification evidence. That result cannot help the guilty avoid conviction but can only help assure that the right man has been brought to justice.

Legislative or other regulations, such as those of local police departments, which eliminate the risks of abuse and unintentional suggestion at lineup proceedings and the impediments to meaningful confrontation at trial may also remove the basis for regarding the stage as "critical." But neither Congress nor the federal authorities have seen fit to provide a solution. . . .

V

We come now to the question whether the denial of Wade's motion to strike the courtroom identification by the bank witnesses at trial because of the absence of his counsel at the lineup required, as the Court of Appeals held, the grant of a new trial at which such evidence is to be excluded. We do not think this disposition can be justified without first giving the Government the opportunity to establish by clear and convincing evidence that the in-court identifications were based upon observations of the suspect other than the lineup identification. Where, as here, the admissibility of evidence of the lineup identification itself is not involved, a *per se* rule of exclusion of courtroom identification would be unjustified. A rule limited solely to the exclusion of testimony concerning identification at the lineup itself, without regard to admissibility of the courtroom identification, would render the right to counsel an empty one. The lineup is most often used, as in the present case, to crystallize the witnesses' identification of the defendant for future reference. We have already noted that the lineup identification will have that effect. The State may then rest upon the witnesses' unequivocal courtroom identification, and not mention the pretrial identification as part of the State's case at trial. Counsel is then in the predicament in which Wade's counsel found himself—realizing that possible unfairness at the lineup may be the sole means of attack upon the unequivocal courtroom identification, and having to probe in the dark in an attempt to discover and reveal unfairness, while bolstering the government witness' courtroom identification by bringing out and dwelling upon his prior identification. Since counsel's presence at the lineup would equip him to attack not only the lineup identification but the courtroom identification as well, limiting the impact of the violation of the right to counsel to exclusion of evidence only of identification at the lineup itself disregards a critical element of that right.

We doubt that the Court of Appeals applied the proper test for exclusion of the in-court identification of the two witnesses. The court stated that "it cannot be said with any certainty that they would have recognized appellant at the time of trial if this intervening lineup had not occurred," and that the testimony of the two witnesses "may well have been colored by the illegal procedure [and] was prejudicial." Moreover, the court was persuaded, in part, by the "compulsory verbal responses made by Wade at the instance of the Special Agent." This implies the erroneous holding that Wade's privilege against self-incrimination was violated so that the denial of counsel required exclusion.

On the record now before us we cannot make the determination whether the in-court identifications had an independent origin. This was not an issue at trial, although there is some evidence relevant to a determination. That inquiry is most properly made in the District Court. We therefore think the appropriate procedure to be followed is to vacate the conviction pending a hearing to determine whether the in-court identifications had an independent source, or whether, in any event, the introduction of the evidence was harmless error, *Chapman* v. *California*, 386 U.S. 18, and for the District Court to reinstate the conviction or order a new trial, as may be proper.

The judgment of the Court of Appeals is vacated and the case is remanded to that court with direction to enter a new judgment vacating the conviction and remanding the case to the District Court for further proceedings consistent with this opinion.

Justice Black dissented in part and concurred in part, saying in part:
. . . I would reverse the Court of Appeals' reversal of Wade's conviction, but I would not remand for further proceedings. Since the prosecution did not use the out-of-court lineup identification against Wade at his trial, I believe the conviction should be affirmed.

I

In rejecting Wade's claim that his privilege against self-incrimination was violated by compelling him to appear in the lineup wearing the tape and uttering the words given him by the police, the Court relies on the recent holding in *Schmerber* v. *California*, 384 U.S. 757. In that case the Court held that taking blood from a man's body against his will in order to convict him of a crime did not compel him to be a witness against himself. The Court's reason for its holding was that the sample of Schmerber's blood taken in order to convict him of crime was neither "testimonial" nor "communicative" evidence. I think it was both. It seems quite plain to me that the Fifth Amendment's Self-incrimination Clause was designed to bar the Government from forcing any person to supply proof of his own crime, precisely what Schmerber was forced to do when he was forced to supply his blood. The Government simply took his blood against his will and over his counsel's protest for the purpose of convicting him of crime. So here, having Wade in its custody awaiting trial to see if he could or would be convicted of crime, the Government forced him to stand in a lineup, wear strips on his face, and speak certain words, in order to make it possible for government witnesses to identify him as a criminal. Had Wade been compelled to utter these or any other words in open court, it is plain that he would have been entitled to a new trial because of having been compelled to be a witness against himself. Being forced by the Government to help convict himself and to supply evidence against himself by talking outside the courtroom is equally violative of his constitutional right not to be compelled to be a witness against himself. Consequently, because of this violation of the Fifth Amendment, and not because of my own personal view that the Government's conduct was "unfair," "prejudicial," or "improper," I would prohibit the prosecution's use of lineup identification at trial.

II

I agree with the Court, in large part because of the reasons it gives, that failure to notify Wade's counsel that Wade was

to be put in a lineup by government officers and to be forced
to talk and wear tape on his face denied Wade the right to
counsel in violation of the Sixth Amendment. . . . [C]ontrary
to the Court, I believe that counsel may advise the defendant
not to participate in the lineup or to participate only under
certain conditions.

I agree with the Court that counsel's presence at the lineup
is necessary to protect the accused's right to a "fair trial," only
if by "fair trial" the Court means a trial in accordance with
the "Law of the Land" as specifically set out in the Constitution. But there are implications in the Court's opinion that
by a "fair trial" the Court means a trial which a majority of
this Court deems to be "fair" and that a lineup is a "critical
state" only because the Court, now assessing the "innumerable dangers" which inhere in it, thinks it is such. That these
implications are justified is evidenced by the Court's suggestion
that "legislative or other regulations . . . which eliminate the
risks of abuse . . . at lineup proceedings . . . may also remove
the basis for regarding the state as 'critical'." . . . I am wholly
unwilling to make the specific constitutional right of counsel
dependent on judges' vague and transitory notions of fairness
and their equally transitory, though thought to be empirical,
assessment of the "risk that . . . counsel's absence . . . might
derogate from . . . a defendant's right to a fair trial."

I would reverse Wade's conviction without further ado had
the prosecution at trial made use of his lineup identification
either in place of courtroom identification or to bolster in a
harmful manner crucial courtroom identification. But the
prosecution here did neither of these things. After prosecution
witnesses under oath identified Wade in the courtroom, it was
the defense, and not the prosecution, which brought out the
prior lineup identification. While stating that "a *per se* rule of
exclusion of courtroom identification would be unjustified,"
the Court, nevertheless, remands this case for "a hearing to
determine whether the in-court identifications had an independent source," or were the tainted fruits of the invalidly
conducted lineup. From this holding I dissent.

In the first place, even if this Court has the power to establish such a rule of evidence, I think the rule fashioned by the Court is unsound. The "tainted fruit" determination required by the Court involves more than considerable difficulty. I think it is practically impossible. How is a witness capable of probing the recesses of his mind to draw a sharp line between a courtroom identification due exclusively to an earlier lineup and a courtroom identification due to memory not based on the lineup? What kind of "clear and convincing evidence" can the prosecution offer to prove upon what particular events memories resulting in an in-court identification rest? How long will trials be delayed while judges turn psychologists to probe the subconscious minds of Witnesses? All these questions are posed but not answered by the Court's opinion. In my view, the Fifth and Sixth Amendments are satisfied if the prosecution is precluded from using lineup identification as either an alternative to or corroboration of courtroom identification. If the prosecution does neither and its witnesses under oath identify the defendant in the courtroom, then I can find no justification for stopping the trial in midstream to hold a lengthy "tainted fruit" hearing. The fact of and circumstances surrounding a prior lineup identification might be used by the defense to impeach the credibility of the in-court identifications, but not to exclude them completely.

But more important, there is no constitutional provision upon which I can rely that directly or by implication gives this Court power to establish what amounts to a constitutional rule of evidence to govern, not only the Federal Government, but the States in their trial of state crimes under state laws in state courts. The Constitution deliberately reposed in the States very broad power to create and to try crimes according to their own rules and policies. Before being deprived of this power, the least that they can ask is that we should be able to point to a federal constitutional provision that either by express language or by necessary implication grants us the power to fashion this novel rule of evidence to govern their criminal trials. . . .

Perhaps the Court presumes to write this constitutional rule of evidence on the basis of the Fourteenth Amendment's Due

Process Clause. This is not the time or place to consider that claim. Suffice it for me to say briefly that I find no such authority in the Due Process Clause. It undoubtedly provides that a person must be tried in accordance with the "Law of the Land." Consequently, it violates the due process to try a person in a way prohibited by the Fourth, Fifth, or Sixth Amendments of our written Constitution. But I have never been able to subscribe to the dogma that the Due Process Clause empowers this Court to declare any law, including a rule of evidence, unconstitutional which it believes is contrary to tradition, decency, fundamental justice, or any of the other wide-meaning words used by judges to claim power under the Due Process Clause. I have an abiding idea that if the Framers had wanted to let judges write the Constitution on any such day-to-day beliefs of theirs, they would have said so instead of so carefully defining their grants and prohibitions in a written constitution. With no more authority than the Due Process Clause I am wholly unwilling to tell the state or federal courts that the United States Constitution forbids them to allow courtroom identification without the prosecution's first proving that the identification does not rest in whole or in part on an illegal lineup. Should I do so, I would feel that we are deciding what the Constitution is, not from what it says, but from what we think it would have been wise for the Framers to put in it. That to me would be "judicial activism" at its worst. I would leave the States and Federal Government free to decide their own rules of evidence. That, I believe, is their constitutional prerogative.

I would affirm Wade's conviction.

Justice White, whom Justice Harlan and Justice Stewart joined dissented in part and concurred in part, saying in part:

The Court has again propounded a broad constitutional rule barring use of a wide spectrum of relevant and probative evidence, solely because a step in its ascertainment or discovery occurs outside the presence of defense counsel. . . .

The Court's opinion is far-reaching. It proceeds first by creating a new *per se* rule of constitutional law: a criminal suspect cannot be subjected to a pretrial identification process in the absence of his counsel without violating the Sixth Amendment. If he is, the State may not buttress a later courtroom identification of the witness by any reference to the previous identification. Furthermore, the courtroom identification is not admissible at all unless the State can establish by clear and convincing proof that the testimony is not the fruit of the earlier identification made in the absence of defendant's counsel—admittedly a heavy burden for the State and probably an impossible one. To all intents and purposes, courtroom identifications are barred if pretrial identifications have occurred without counsel being present.

The rule applies to any lineup, to any other techniques employed to produce an identification and *a fortiori* to a face-to-face encounter between the witness and the suspect alone, regardless of when the identification occurs, in time or place, and whether before or after indictment or information. It matters not how well the witness knows the suspect, whether the witness is the suspect's mother, brother, or long-time associate, and no matter how long or well the witness observed the perpetrator at the scene of the crime. The kidnap victim who has lived for days with his abductor is in the same category as the witness who has had only a fleeting glimpse of the criminal. Neither may identify the suspect without defendant's counsel being present. The same strictures apply regardless of the number of other witnesses who positively identify the defendant and regardless of the corroborative evidence showing that it was the defendant who had committed the crime.

The premise for the Court's rule is not the general unreliability of eyewitness identifications nor the difficulties inherent in observation, recall, and recognition. The Court assumes a narrower evil as the basis for its rule—improper police suggestion which contributes to erroneous identifications. The Court apparently believes that improper police procedures are so widespread that a broad prophylactic rule must be laid down, requiring the presence of counsel at all pretrial identifications, in order to detect recurring instances of police misconduct. I do not share this pervasive distrust of all official investigations. None of the materials the Court relies upon supports it. . . .

The Court goes beyond assuming that a great majority of the country's police departments are following improper practices at pretrial identifications. To find the lineup a "critical" stage of the proceeding and to exclude identifications made in the absence of counsel, the Court must also assume that police "suggestion," if it occurs at all, leads to erroneous rather than accurate identifications and that reprehensible police conduct will have an unavoidable and largely undiscoverable impact on the trial. This in turn assumes that there is now no adequate sources from which defense counsel can learn about the circumstances of the pretrial identification in order to place before the jury all of the considerations which should enter into an appraisal of courtroom identification evidence. But these are treacherous and unsupported assumptions, resting as they do on the notion that the defendant will not be aware, that the police and the witnesses will forget or prevaricate, that defense counsel will be unable to bring out the truth that neither jury, judge, nor appellate court is a sufficient safeguard against unacceptable police conduct occurring at a pretrial identification procedure. I am unable to share the Court's view of the willingness of the police and the ordinary citizen-witness to dissemble, either with respect to the identification of the defendant or with respect to the circumstances surrounding a pretrial identification.

There are several striking aspects to the Court's holding. First, the rule does not bar courtroom identifications where there have been no previous identifications in the presence of the police, although when identified in the courtroom, the defendant is known to be in custody and charged with the commission of a crime. Second, the Court seems to say that if suitable legislative standards were adopted for the conduct of pretrial identifications, thereby lessening the hazards in such confrontations, it would not insist on the presence of counsel. But if this is true, why does not the Court simply fashion what it deems to be constitutionally acceptable procedures for the authorities to follow? Certainly the Court is correct in suggesting that the new rule will be wholly inapplicable where police departments themselves have established suitable safeguards.

Third, courtroom identification may be barred, absent counsel at a prior identification, regardless of the extent of counsel's information concerning the circumstances of the previous confrontation between witness and defendant—apparently even if there were recordings or sound-movies of the events as they occurred. But if the rule is premised on the defendant's right to have his counsel know, there seems little basis for not accepting other means to inform. A disinterested observer, recordings, photographs—any one of them would seem adequate to furnish the basis for a meaningful cross-examination of the eyewitness who identifies the defendant in the courtroom.

. . . Beyond this, however, requiring counsel at pretrial identifications as an invariable rule trenches on other valid state interests. One of them is its concern with the prompt and efficient enforcement of its criminal laws. Identifications frequently take place after arrest but before an indictment is returned or an information is filed. The police may have arrested a suspect on probable cause but may still have the wrong man. Both the suspect and the State have every interest in a prompt identification at that stage, the suspect in order to secure his immediate release and the State because prompt and early identification enhances *accurate* identification and because it must know whether it is on the right investigative track. Unavoidably, however, the absolute rule requiring the presence of counsel will cause significant delay and it may very well result in no pretrial identification at all. Counsel must be appointed and a time arranged convenient for him and the witnesses. Meanwhile, it may be necessary to file charges against the suspect who may then be released on bail, in the federal system very often on his own recognizance, with neither the State nor the defendant having the benefit of a properly conducted identification procedure.

Nor do I think the witnesses themselves can be ignored. They will now be required to be present at the convenience of counsel rather than their own. Many may be much less willing to participate if the identification stage is transformed into an adversary proceeding not under the control of a judge. Others may fear for their own safety if their identity is known at an early date, especially when there is no way of knowing until the lineup occurs whether or not the police really have the right man.

Finally, I think the Court's new rule is vulnerable in terms of its own unimpeachable purpose of increasing the reliability of identification testimony.

Law enforcement officers have the obligation to convict the guilty and to make sure they do not convict the innocent. They must be dedicated to making the criminal trial a procedure for the ascertainment of the true facts surrounding the commission of the crime. To this extent, our so-called adversary system is not adversary at all; nor should it be. But defense counsel has no comparable obligation to ascertain or present the truth. Our system assigns him a different mission. He must be and is interested in preventing the conviction of the innocent, but, absent a voluntary plea of guilty, we also insist that he defend his client whether he is innocent or guilty. The State has the obligation to present the evidence. Defense counsel need present nothing, even if he knows what the truth is. He need not furnish any witnesses to the police, or reveal any confidences of his client, or furnish any other information to help the prosecution's case. If he can confuse a witness, even a truthful one, or make him appear at a disadvantage, unsure or indecisive, that will be his normal course. Our interest in not convicting the innocent permits counsel to put the State to its proof, to put the State's case in the worst possible light, regardless of what he thinks or knows to be the truth. Undoubtedly there are some limits which defense counsel must observe but more often than not, defense counsel will cross-examine a prosecution witness, and impeach him if he can, even if he thinks the witness is telling the truth, just as he will attempt to destroy a witness who he thinks is lying. In this respect, as part of our modified adversary system and as part of the duty imposed on the most honorable defense counsel, we countenance or require conduct which in many instances has little, if any, relation to the search for truth.

I would not extend this system, at least as it presently operates, to police investigations and would not require counsel's presence at pretrial identification procedures. Counsel's interest is in not having his client placed at the scene of the crime, regardless of his whereabouts. Some counsel may advise their clients to refuse to make any movements or to speak any words in a lineup or even to appear in one. To that extent the impact on truth factfinding is quite obvious. . . . In my view, the State is entitled to investigate and develop its case outside the presence of defense counsel. This includes the right to have private conversations with identification witnesses, just as defense counsel may have his own consultations with these and other witnesses without having the prosecutor present.

Whether today's judgment would be an acceptable exercise of supervisory power over federal courts is another question. But as a constitutional matter, the judgment in this case is erroneous and although I concur in Parts I and III of the Court's opinion I respectfully register this dissent.

Justice Fortas, with whom the Chief Justice and Justice Douglas joined, concurred in part and dissented in part, saying in part:

1. I agree with the Court that the exhibition of the person of the accused at a lineup is not itself a violation of the privilege against self-incrimination. In itself, it is no more subject to constitutional objection than the exhibition of the person of the accused in the courtroom for identification purposes. . . . It is, however, a "critical stage" in the prosecution, and I agree with the Court that the opportunity to have counsel present must be made available.

2. In my view, however, the accused may not be compelled in a lineup to speak the words uttered by the person who committed the crime. I am confident that it could not be compelled in court. It cannot be compelled in a lineup. . . .

I completely agree that the accused must be advised of and given the right to counsel before a line-up—and I join in that part of the Court's opinion; but this is an empty right unless we mean to insist upon the accused's fundamental constitutional immunities. One of these is that the accused may not be compelled to speak. To compel him to speak would violate the privilege against self-incrimination, which is incorporated in the Fifth Amendment. . . .

An accused cannot be compelled to utter the words spoken by the criminal in the course of the crime. I thoroughly disagree with the Court's statement that such compulsion does not violate the Fifth Amendment. . . .

Accordingly, while I join the Court in requiring vacating of the judgment below. . . . I would do so not only because of the failure to offer counsel before the lineup but also because of the violation of respondent's Fifth Amendment rights.

LIBRARY OF DAVIDSON COLLEGE

Books on regular loan may be checked out for **two weeks**. Books must be presented at the Circulation Desk in order to be renewed.

A fine of **five cents** a day is charged after date due.

Special books are subject to special regulations at the discretion of library staff.

AUG. 30, 1974					
NOV. -5, 1975					
NOV 19, 1975					
DEC -6, 1975					
MAR. 11, 1976					
DEC -1, 1978					
JAN. 11, 1979					
MAR. 11, 1980					